MINIATURE LAMPS-II

MINIATURE LAMPS-II

Revised & Expanded 2nd Edition

by Ruth Smith

Schiffer Publishing Ltd ®

4880 Lower Valley Road, Atglen, PA 19310 USA

Dedication

IN LOVING MEMORY OF MY DEAR HUSBAND FRANK, WHO MADE MY COLLECTION OF MINIA-TURE LAMPS AND FIRST BOOK POSSIBLE.

Revised price guide: 2000
Copyright © 1982 & 2000 by Ruth E. Smith.
Library of Congress Catalog Card Number: 00-100613

Typeset in Aldine 721 BT

ISBN: 0-7643-1094-1
Printed in China
1 2 3 4

Published by Schiffer Publishing Ltd.
4880 Lower Valley Road
Atglen, PA 19310
Phone: (610) 593-1777; Fax: (610) 593-2002
E-mail: Schifferbk@aol.com
Please visit our web site catalog at
www.schifferbooks.com

We are always looking for authors to write books on new and related subjects. If you have an idea for a book please contact us at the address above. This book may be purchased from the publisher.
Include $3.95 for shipping. Please try your bookstore first.
You may write for a free printed catalog.

In Europe, Schiffer books are distributed by
Bushwood Books
6 Marksbury Avenue
Kew Gardens
Surrey TW9 4JF England
Phone: 44 (0)208-392-8585; Fax: 44 (0)208-392-9876
E-mail: Bushwd@aol.com
Free postage in the UK., Europe; air mail at cost.

Acknowledgments

Before my husband died in September 1979, he photographed lamps different from any of those in *Miniature Lamps* book I.

Having these photographs in my possession I decided to do something with them. I contacted collectors of miniature lamps asking if they would cooperate with me in helping to put out another book on miniature lamps, needless to say, their response was great. Combining the photographs they supplied me with the photographs I had, this is how *Miniature Lamps* book II was made possible.

My appreciation and sincerest thanks to Mr. Albert Christian Revi, Hanover, Pennsylvania, for helping in the preparation of Miniature Lamps book II.

Also, my special thanks and appreciation goes to the collectors of miniature lamps who willingly contributed their time and effort in having photographs made and sent to me of their lamps, making it possible for *Miniature Lamps II*. Without their whole-hearted cooperation I could not have done this alone. To each and every one of those wonderful collectors of miniature lamps, I shall always be grateful and I thank them from the "bottom of my heart".

Mrs. Fred C. Bartel, 425 South Buffalo Street, Warsaw, Indiana; Mr. and Mrs. Guy Bailey, Hooker, Oklahoma; Dorla and Bud Battersby, 651 Shahar Avenue, Lone Pine, California; Marion and Chuck Berryman, El Cajon, California; Dorlores A. Burke, Virginia Beach, Virginia; Mr. and Mrs. Carlton L. Cotting, Vienna, Virginia; Mr. and Mrs. Don Carman, Columbus, Georgia; Captain and Mrs. C. T. Creekman, 5001 Newsome Circle, Virginia Beach, Virginia; Mr. and Mrs. William D. Caskey, Stockridge, Michigan; Mrs. Mary Jane Clark, 52444 Laurel Road, south Bend, Indiana; Mrs. Camille Cox, 8344 San Cristabal, Dallas, Texas; Mr. and Mrs. John Duris, Riveredge 33, Ivoryton, Connecticut; Ione Ellis, La Mesa, California; Mr. and Mrs. Joseph Ford, 607 Melvin Road, Telford, Pennsylvania; Mr. and Mrs. Wilbur Feltner, Box 2286, Winchester, Virginia; Marjorie Hulsebus,

Glendale, California; Mr. and Mrs. Robert W. Kerns, Route 3, Box 63, Berkely Springs, West Virginia; Mr. and Mrs. George Lemon, 946 Noland Drive, Hagerstown, Maryland; Mr. and Mrs. Franklin Lennox, 2627 South Drive, Adrian, Michigan; Mr. and Mrs. Hugo von Linden, 109 Grand Street, Schoharie, New York; The late Mr. Myers; Mr. and Mrs. Thomas Miller, Des Moines, Iowa; Mr. and Mrs. Frank L. McWright, 21 Pell Mell Drive, Bethel, Connecticut; Ann Gilbert McDonald, Arlington, Virginia; Mr. and Mrs. John Ness, 743 Conewago Avenue, York, Pennsylvania; Mr. and Mrs. Walt Oswald, Aurora, Nebraska; Mr. and Mrs. Harry T. Plasterer, 17 Clover Avenue, Strasburg, Pennsylvania; Mr. and Mrs. Arthur A. Ronat, Mr. Vernon, Illinois; Mr. and Mrs. Richard J. Rosenberger, 420 Briarmont Drive, Winchester, Virignia; Mr. and Mrs. John g. Rapai, 5800 South Rockwood Road, Rockwood, Michigan; Mr. and Mrs. Joseph Reith Jr., 508 East Poplar, Kokomo, Indiana; Mr. and Mrs. Ernest Rodney, Exton, Pennsylvania; Lynne and Jack Robinson, El Cajon, California; Mr. and Mrs. Elmer L. Ritter, 306 Candle Light Drive, Camp Hill, Pennsylvania; Roan's Auction House, Williamsport, Pennsylvania, for allowing the Boles lamps to be photographed before being sold; Mr. and Mrs. Richard F. Shroyock, 145 Cheswold Lane, Haverford, Pennsylvania; Dr. Ed Sensel, 105 East First Street, Corning, New York; Dr. John F. Solverson, P.O. Box 439, Rochester, Michigan; Mr. and Mrs. Dick Semprini, 200 Walco Road, Bristol, Connecticut; Mrs. Sadie Smith, West Central, Wisconsin; Bob Schafer, 1119 North Vinedo Avenue, Pasadena, California; Mr. and Mrs. Tom Stewart III, 15 Charles Street, New York; Mrs. Helen Sandeen, Falls Church, Virginia; Mr. and Mrs. Harold Shipman, 809 Lafayette Parkway, Williamsport, Pennsylvania; Mr. and Mrs. Clinton Terrio, 775 Cedar Street, Elmira, New York; Mr. and Mrs. Martin J. Whele, 46 Stottle Road, Churchville, New York; Mr. and Mrs. Herbert White, Route 1, Box 151, Sherman, Connecticut; Leona Willis, 4975 North Main Street, Balwin Park, California.

Foreword

Even before the first edition of *Miniature Lamps* came off the presses in 1968, Frank and Ruth Smith were photographing, measuring and researching newly found lamps purchased for their own extensive collection, or discovered in another collector's possession. They traveled far and wide to visit fellow collectors and see their miniature lamps. On the other hand, collectors from all over the country cam to their home in Pennsylvania to view a remarkable assemblage of tiny lamps in the ever-growing collection of the Smiths.

Through all of this, friendships were made and information exchanged. Both new and old friends supplied photographs of lamps from their collections that the Smiths had never seen before. The result was a collection of more than six hundred photographs of miniature lamps not illustrated in the Smiths first book. What else could they do, but share these newly found treasures with other collectors. And this is how *Miniature Lamps—Book Two* came to be.

In keeping with the format of their first book, lamps found in more than one color or kind of glass have been noted in the captions. This does not mean, however, that these same lamps cannot be found in still other colors or kinds of glass.

The measurements given are to the top of the lamp shade—not the chimney. These measurements will vary somewhat depending on the kind of burner used, or the angle at which the arms of the tripod shade support are bent. Lamps having no shades have been measured to the top of the brass collar.

Careful attention has been give to insure that the shades shown with the bases are original to these lamps and not a replacement, either old or new. Many of the lamps have been identified through illustrations of miniature lamps found in old catalogs and trade journals.

Frank Smith passed away before this book was in its final stages. But his contribution is manifested in several of the photographs of miniature lamps he took over a period of more than ten years. Collectors owe him and his wife a debt of gratitude for their steadfast pursuit of other kinds of miniature lamps, and their scholarly and continued research in this field of collecting.

Albert Christian Revi, Editor
Spinning Wheel

Annapolis, Maryland
February 1982

Foreword
2nd Edition

Miniature Lamps II is a pictorial guide for both the beginner and the advanced collector. The variety of these tiny treasures is endless. One collector may enjoy primitives, while another may indulge themselves in exquisite art glass.

Book II has been updated to include an estimated value for each of the lamps. These values are based on recent antique showings, estate sales, and reputable dealers. Prices of miniature lamps vary in different parts of the country and also depend on the abundance, scarcity, and the condition of the lamps. Small imperfections are expected, but large chips and cracks will lower the values significantly.

There are several ways to locate auctions or sales on miniature lamps. Subscribing to antique publications such as Antique Week, The Antique Trader, and Antiques and Auction News are excellent sources of information. Well known auction houses that specialize in miniature lamps are Roan Bros. Auction Gallery, RR 4, Box 118, Cogan Station, PA 17728, and James D. Julia, Inc., PO Box 830, Fairfield, ME 04937. Auction houses such as these mentioned are great sources of information on past auctions as well as a channel through which to purchase lamps in the future.

All prices quoted in the updated Miniature Lamps II are intended only as a guide and not warranted as to accuracy. No responsibility, liability, losses, or other errors incurred by the buyer, seller, or anyone else will be assumed by the writers or the publishers.

Joanne Rumbley
March 2000

Contents

Manufacturers' Advertisements

The following advertisements represent the wide variety of promotional material which appeared in manufacturers' sales catalogs of the last decade of the 19th century and early 20th century. from these widely circulated catalogs, store owners throughout the country ordered the lamps for their stores. Thereby, national distribution was achieved.

From "Out Drummer" catalog, Butler Brothers, New York. February, 1900 issue.

302, "Heart Pattern" Night Lamp—A large pure crystal little lamp of rare lines of beauty, 9¼ inches high. Has burner, chimney and wick complete. ½ doz. in box

1241, "Eagle" Colored Night Lamp Handy shape. Assorted green, canary and maroon, tinted and gold decorations, 8 in. high, each box, complete burner, chimney, wick, 4 inch globe shade

25, "Elephant" Opal Night Lamp Lamp represents an elephant kneeling, size 5 inches, caparison and houdah painted in rich colors and gold, complete with brass burner, globe ring, tall chimney and globe decorated to match. Full height 9¼ inches. Each in pkg

From "Out Drummer" catalog, Butler Brothers, New York. February, 1900 issue.

12

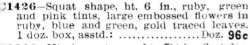

C1426—Squat shape, ht. 6 in., ruby, green and pink tints, large embossed flowers in ruby, blue and green, gold traced leaves. 1 doz. box, asstd.: ....Doz. **96c**

C1210—Mission octagon, ht. 7¼ in., 6 styles. 3 shades, 3 globes, pink, green canary and blended colors, jet black panel formations. 1 in carton. ½ doz. pkg. ....Doz. **$1.75**

C1219—8¾ in., pink, yellow and green decorations, opal, black stripes, colored poppies and leaves, nkl. foot and trim. 1 in carton. ....Doz. **$2.15**

C1215—Ht. 10¼, paneled globe and body in Kopp's famous colors, all over satin etched, ⅓ cardinal red, and ⅔ pink. 1 in carton, 6 in pkg. ....Each, **37c**

Grocers' edition of "Our Drummer". Butler Brothers, 495-497 Broadway, New York. Spring April 30, 1912. Catalog number 975A. Exclusive wholesalers of general merchandise.

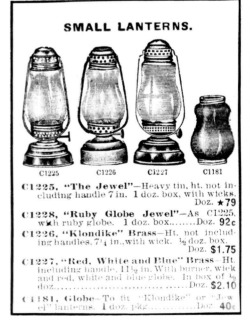

SMALL LANTERNS.

C1225. **"The Jewel"**—Heavy tin, ht. not including handle 7 in. 1 doz. box, with wicks. Doz. **★79**

C1228. **"Ruby Globe Jewel"**—As C1225, with ruby globe. 1 doz. box.......Doz. **92c**

C1226. **"Klondike" Brass**—Ht. not including handles, 7¼ in., with wick. ½ doz. box. Doz. **$1.75**

C1227. **"Red, White and Blue" Brass**—Ht. including handle, 11½ in. With burner, wick and red, white and blue globe. In box of ½ doz. ....Doz. **$2.10**

C1181. **Globe**—To fit "Klondike" or "Jewel" lanterns. 1 doz. pkg. ....Doz. **40c**

13

C1206   C1425   C1207   C1203

C2569   C1421   C1424

C1206—6½ in., embossed base and bowl, pink, blue and green opal, gilt divisions. 1 doz. box.. .... Doz. **93c**

C1425—6½ in., mission design, pink, yellow and green opal, black divisions. Doz. **95c**

C1207—"Daisy." Footed, ht. 9, best crystal glass, large bulls eye foot and shoulder, colonial stem. ½ doz. box.........Doz. **95c**

C1203—Crystal, ribbed base, square shaped foot, plain fount, handsome pattern, purest crystal. 1doz. box. ....Doz. **96c**

C2569 — 9¼ in., 1 piece, plain, ruby, gree[n] and crystal foot, octagon fluted chimne[y,] ⅔ doz., each 3 patterns, 2 doz. case. Doz. **92**

C1421—Ht. 6¾, footed, pink, green and ye[l-] low tinted opal, embossed colored grape[s] and gilt leaf vine. 1 doz. box......Doz. **92**

C1424—7½ in., pink, yellow and green opa[l,] red and gold decorated grapevine emboss[-] ing. 1 doz. box......................Doz. **92**

C1220   C1221   C1222

C1220, "Star"—Handled, metal lacquered, fount, asstd. red, green and violet. Complete with nutmeg burner, wick and chimney. 1 doz. box, asstd. colors... .... Doz. **82c**

C1221, "Nevertip" — Full ht. 7 in., wide fount, brass gem burner, wick and chimney. 1 doz. box...........................Doz. **92c**

C1222, Brass Handled — Brilliant lacquered brass, ht. 7, diam. 4. Complete with "Gem" burner, wick and chimney. ½ doz. box. Doz. **$1.20**

"SOUTHERN" BRASS HAND LAMP.

C1224 — Large size, *lacquered brass fount*, brass fluid ratchet burner and round wick used without chimney. 1 doz. box with wicks. Doz. **96c**

Grocers' edition of "Our Drummer". Butler Brothers, 495-497 Broadway, New York. Spring April 30, 1912. Catalog number 975A. Exclusive wholesalers of general merchandise.

C. M. Livingston's Silent salesman. 207-209 Madison Street, Chicago, IL. January, 1894. Complete edition.

IDAHO NIGHT LAMP.

The Latest and Most Attractive Bargain.

Idaho Night Lamp. Very handsome, new design, heavy bisque finish glass footed standard and dome shade, elegantly embellished with raised floral designs, finely finished nickel-plated trimmings, complete with wick and chimney. This is, in fact a miniature parlor shade lamp; stands 8 inches high, and is perfect in every detail. Put up 1 dozen in a package. Price per dozen.................. 4.35

SPECIAL LEADERS.

Our "Little Beauty" Night Lamp. A handsome new style, made of heavy porcelain finished glass, heavily footed, good size fount, fancy pattern, scalloped top edges, pendant shell decorations, hand painted vines and flowers between the shell in contrasting colors, good burner, globe chimney to match fount. Height of lamp, complete, 10 inches, fount 11¼ inches in circumference, globe chimney 10½ inches in circumference. This makes a beautiful half-dollar bargain. Packed one dozen in a box. Price per dozen................... 3.12

No. 1683. Little Royal Lamp. Made entirely of metal, handsomely embossed fount, ornamental foot, adjustable tripod, patent drip cup, outside feeder wick, central draft tube, absolutely non-explosive. Heavily nickel plated. Very handsome embossed pattern, central draft, complete with wick, chimney and shade. A neat bedroom or kitchen lamp.

Little Beauty.   No. 1863.

Finished in Polished Brass....... .... 7.13
Finished in Nickel. 7.68
Finished in Bronze.................. .... 7.80

NIGHT LAMPS.

No. 4 Handled Brass Night Lamp. One dozen in a box. Takes No. 0 or 1 burner. Without chimney .....10.15   .87

No. 2 Handled Night Lamp. One dozen in a box, assorted founts: blue, opal and flint, wire handle, complete with burner, chimney and wick....•..........—— 1.41

No. 4.   No. 2.   No. 3.

No. 3 Nickel Plated Brass Night Lamp. One-half dozen in a box. Nicely finished. Complete with burner, wick and chimney ....—— 1.68

C. M. Livingston's Silent salesman. 207-209 Madison Street, Chicago, IL. January, 1894. Complete edition.

C. M. Livingston's Silent salesman. 207-209 Madison Street, Chicago, IL. January, 1894. Complete edition.

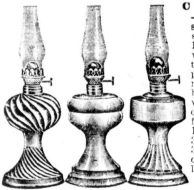

Kenova Night Lamp

Miniature lamps made by the Fostoria Glass Company. West Virginia, Ca. 1890. Top: "Kenova Night Lamp," Bottom: "Excell Night Lamp."

17

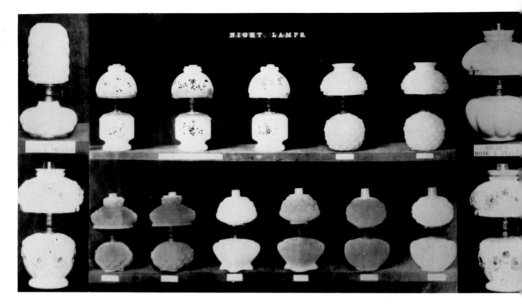

Miniature lamps made by the Westmoreland Specialty Company, Grapeville, PA. Ca. 1890. Top row; "Acme" (rose and yellow); "Sylvan" (with assorted decorations); "No. 800"; Bottom row; "Daisy" "Cosmos Pattern" (now called the opal with painted decorations. "Basket" (found in rose and yellow); "Rose" (made in a variety of colors with a satin finish); "No. 02" "Daisy" (the Cosmos Pattern).

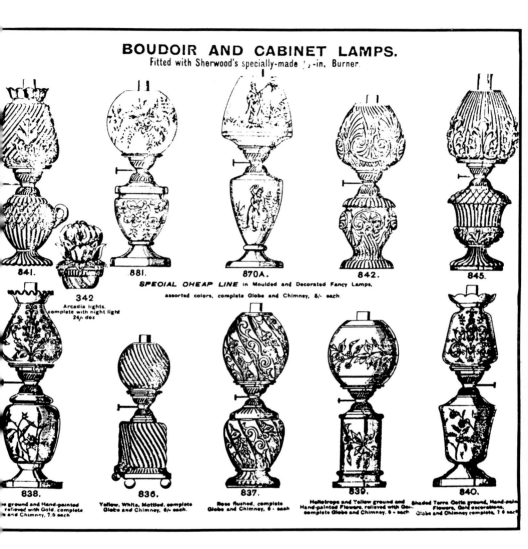

Boudior and Cabinet Lamps from an undated and unidentified English Catalog,
Ca. 1880. *Courtesy of Mike Parker.*

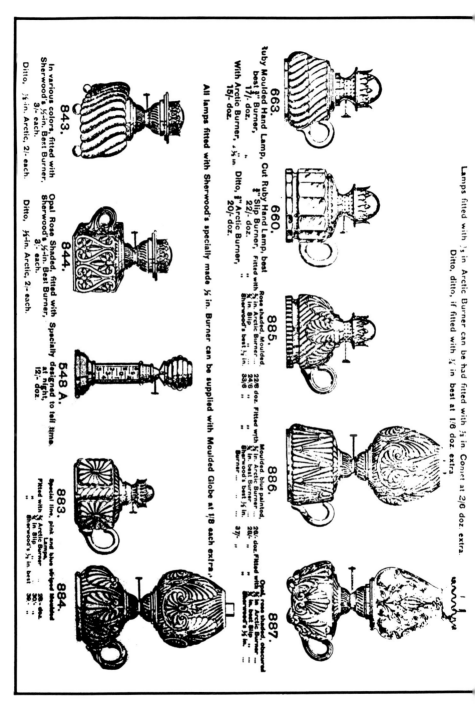

Boudior and Cabinet Lamps from an undated and unidentified English Catalog, Ca. 1880. *Courtesy of Mike Parker.*

The Historical Development of the Miniature Lamp

Development of Miniature Lamps

Night or miniature oil lamps are replicas in miniature of the oil lamps that were in use before electric lights were available. By this we do not mean that every type or pattern of miniature lamp had a larger counterpart. While there is no hard and fast rule, perhaps a reasonable definition of a miniature or junior-sized lamp would be one that is too small to give adequate reading light for the period when it was made and used.

A lamp around twelve inches to the top of the shade is usually considered as miniature although many of them are much smaller. Above this size, smaller editions of large ornamental lamps are often referred to as junior-sized lamps. This includes the smaller copies of banquet lamps which are often called miniatures because they are so much smaller than their larger counterparts.

Glass miniature lamps appeared at an early date. Among the first items made at Sandwich were lamps, mentioned as early as July 30, 1825, less than a month after the factory opened. Some of these may well have been miniatures. They were sperm- or whale-oil lamps and were made to be used by burning the string-like wicks which were thrust through tubes in a cork. As various changes and improvements were made in lamps, miniature copies kept pace with the larger ones. As a matter of fact, many of the regularly used whale-oil lamps were so small as to be almost miniatures. Today small lamps with either the whale-oil or champhene type of burner are considered by most collectors as early lights and a collection to themselves.

In the 1850s, glass chimneys to enclose and protect the flame began to appear on lamps using kerosene. It is said that the lamp chimney was invented when a workman was heating a bottle over an open flame. The bottom of the bottle snapped off and the workman noticed how much brighter and more evenly the flame burned when the bottomless bottle was held over it. This may be the true origin of the modern lamp chimney. However, as we have seen, Leonardo da Vinci had used a chimney for protecting the flame centuries before.

Several different types of burners were soon developed to improve the burning and illuminating qualities of the lamps using the new fuel. The standard burner for miniature oil lamps was patented by L. J. Atwood on February 27, 1877. Shortly afterward, on March 20 and April 24, 1877, L. H. Olmsted patented another type of burner. The Olmsted burner is often called the Sandwich burner because it is often found in miniature Sandwich lamps. The development of these burners made possible the real beginning of miniature lamps as they are known and collected today.

The first miniature oil lamps were simple and utilitarian in construction. Soon, however, a shade was added to enclose and protect the chimney and, in reality, to add beauty to the lamp. As the beautiful parlor lamps of the late Victorian age were developed, the miniature lamp also became more beautiful and elaborate. Almost every type of art glass known at the time appears in these lamps. It was indeed their golden age. It is these lamps that are so eagerly sought by collectors at the present time.

As oil lamps became obsolete some miniature electric lamps were made. Tiffany made some small electric lamps similar to those he made for candles and oil. In Europe some beautiful electric millefiore and cameo miniatures were produced, but judging by their scarcity, they were not numerous. Although much safer and more satisfactory than oil lamps, the miniature electric lamps never became popular in the country. In recent years some of the oil miniatures have been converted for electricity.

In recent years the miniature oil lamp has stage a comeback in popularity. Many beautiful little lamps may now be found in both glass and porcelain in art and gift shops. Many of these are imports, but some are of domestic manufacture. It is to be regretted that some antique dealers handle these and through ignorance or greed, offer them as old at fantastic prices. Recently such a dealer offered one to us for $135.00. At a nearby gift shop similar lamps were available for $7.50.

The Use of Miniature Lamps

Miniature lamps were used for a number of purposes, but some dealers and collectors champion one or another of these uses to the exclusion of all the others. In most old catalogs they are referred to as "night lamps," which really tells little as to their use but leaves the buyer to use his purchase as he sees fit.

As night lights they were doubtless often used as a dim light to burn through the night after the big lamps had been extinguished. They would also make good lights for sick rooms, for the elderly, or for children's rooms.

We have a stereopticon card (see page 21), with the copyright date of 1899, showing two little girls I their bedroom preparing to retire. On a table by the bed is a miniature lamp like that shown in *Fig.* 296 book I. Doubtless a child would feel safe and secure with the soft light of such a lamp to frighten away bogey men and other such "dangers" that might creep up in the dark.

A Stereopticon card of 1899 showing a "Sylvan" miniature lamp; put out by Keystone View Company, Meadville, Pa. We wish to thank the company for permission to reproduce this picture. See also *Fig. 296* book I.

9477—Undergoing Repairs.

Doubtless many of the little lamps were given to children for their rooms or playhouses. I, myself, had two of the little lamps in my playhouse, and years later these two were the foundation on which our collection was based. Somewhere we have seen an advertisement of a special oil can showing a mother filling a large parlor lamp while by her side stands a little girl holding her miniature lamp to be filled.

The Time and Light (*Fig.* 23 book I) could be placed by the bed, and if the sleeper awakened during the night the oil level in the lamp would tell the time. One of our friends tested the lamp and found that it was surprisingly accurate when equipped with the original burner and string-like wick. Some of these lamps are now found equipped with nutmeg burners with the flat wicks. Such lamps have lost their utility as timepieces.

Some people claim that these time lamps were courting lamps, lighted when the beau arrived at eight in the evening, and used to time his visit. Perhaps this is true, but since the lamps tells time for ten hours (from eight until six) it seems more probable that it was a night lamp. In those days, early to bed and early to rise was the rule, while a suitor who lingered until six in the morning would certainly have been frowned upon by any strict parent.

Some claim that all miniatures were courting lamps to be used in the parlor when the young lady of the hose had a caller. Doubtless one of these beautiful lamps would add an aura of charm and romance, while the dim light would answer all the requirements of propriety for lovers.

The miniatures may also have served as salesmen's samples to show the prospective purchasers what the standard-sized lamps were like. We have had antique dealers tell us the original owners, from whom they purchased the lamp, said that it was a drummer's sample given to them or some of their relatives. Comparatively few of the miniature lamps, however, have larger counterparts, so this premise seems unfounded. Possibly such lamps were given to retailers who gave the drummer a substantial order. In at least one case (*Fig.* 270 book I), a clothier in Washington, Pennsylvania, gave these little lamps to his customers, possibly in place of calendars at Christmas.

Lastly, since many of the lamps were beautifully made of the finest and most colorful glass, they were ornaments in their own right. At the time of their manufacture, the late Victorian and Gay 90s period, they would have fitted right into the elaborately decorated surroundings. Many of the most beautiful examples show little if any signs of use so that some were probably bought and used on ly as ornaments.

The Component Parts of a Miniature Lamp

Even the most simply constructed miniature lamp is composed of several separate parts. From a study of these parts it is sometimes possible to determine the age of the lamp, the country of origin, and also if the lamp is all original.

The collector must not loose sight of the fact that over the years burners may have been changed or that chimneys have been broken and replaced. He must remember that there is little information on just how most lamps were originally equipped. A Nutmeg lamp, which was made in America, with a foreign burner has obviously been tampered with, but in many cases the collector will have to rely on his own experience and judgement in forming his opinion. We will give a few observations on the various parts of the lamps in the hopes that they will be found interesting and helpful.

The Base. The base or oil font with the attached collar is often all that remains of a lamp. Many bases so found are then provided with burners and chimneys and some people assure the customer that th elamp is complete. In the case of many hand lamps and stem lamps this is true, but with most fancy bases the collector should be skeptical. It must not be forgotten that it is very difficult to find a matching shade for such a base and an incomplete lamp is of limited value to a serious collector.

Collars. Collars are the metal caps, usually of brass, on top of the font into which the burners are screwed. The most common type on both the miniature and standard-sized lamps fits loosely over an elevated lip molded on top of the font. They were originally attached with plaster of Paris, but some are now found fastened on with putty. This appears to be the collar patented by George W. Brown of Forestville, Connecticut, on March 21, 1876, although some are marked "Pat'd Apr. 13, 1876 & Mch. 21, 1878." This type of miniature collar is about an inch in diameter, and takes either an Acourn or a Nutmeg burner. Most have nearly straight side but others have sloping sides or flare out at the bottom. Some are very plain, others are variously ornamented with rings or knurls. Some, that appear to be of late manufacture, screw onto threads molded on the top of the glass font. We have never noticed patent dates or manufactures' names on any of these late collars.

Another type of collar that also takes the Nutmeg and Acorn burners appears to be rather rare. It consists of a narrow band of brass (7/8 of an inch in diameter) embedded in the glass at the top of the font. In the glass around some of these is embossed in very small and indistinct letters' "Patented Sept. 19 & Nov. 14, 1911." Some have no such marking. We have never seen this collar in any except the small size.

Collars for the Hornet-sized burners are made in the same way as the smaller sizes. They are about one and a half inches in diameter. Collars for standard-sized lamps are but larger editions of those for small lamps.

Collars attached with plaster of Paris were apparently rarely replaced on lamps. If the plaster of paris gave way, the collar was reattached rather than being replaced by a new one.

A third type of collar is also about one and a half inches in diameter, and is screwed onto the threaded top of the glass font instead of being permanently attached with plaster of Paris. This type takes the Nutmeg and Acorn burners. Some of these screw-top bases were also equipped with perforated tops and put out in pairs as salt and pepper shakers. That they were also originally put out as lamps is proved by the fact that some types have matching globe-chimney shades. Others have only the burner and chimney and apparently never had a matching shade.

Somewhat similar lamps with a two-inch screw-on collar are also found. They take either the Nutmeg and Acorn or the Hornet burner. These collars are often of tin rather then of brass, and the lamps are pressed glass and rather cheap looking. They have matching globe or umbrella shade or, in the case of the Hornet burner, a globe-chimney shade. We have never seen these bases equipped with shaker tops.

There are several other collars that differ somewhat from those described but it does not seem worthwhile to give details for all of them. Foreign collars are generally very similar to those made in America. The screw-on type of collar seems to be rare in foreign lamps except on those of very recent manufacture.

Burners. Five types of burners of American manufacture are found on miniature lamps. The thre most commonly found, the Nutmeg, the Acorn, and the Hornet, were all made by the Plume and Atwood Manufacturing Company of Waterbury, Connecticut, under Patent #187,800, which was issued February 27, 1877, to L.J. Atwood, and assigned to the company. This company also made the Victor burner fo rjunior-sized lamps. This burner resembles European burners for the same type of lamps. They also made burners similar to the Olmstead for very small lamps. These burners seem to have had no specific name on them, at least we found none marked. It may be that unmarked burners, or those marked only by stars or other ornaments, were made by other companies.

Nutmeg burners are variously marked on the wheel of the wick raiser. What appears to be older ones are marked "Pat. Feb'y 27, 1877." Others, probably of later manufacture, are marked "P & A Mfg. Co.," Made in U.S.A." or ornamented with a twelve-pointed star design. A silver burner on a lamp ornamented with silver filigree is marked "E.M. & Co."

Recently-made burners are marked "The P. & A. Mfg. Co. Acorn"; they resemble the old Nutmeg burners in shape.

The Acorn burners are also variously marked. What appears to be older ones are marked "The P. & A. Mfg. Co. Acorn." Others are ornamented with a circle of six dots, while others are plain with no marks or ornaments whatsoever.

Both the Nutmeg and Acorn burners take either a ring for the ball and upturned shades, or a tripod for umbrella shades. These fixtures come separately but slip down over the ring of prongs which holds the chimney. In older burners a distinct ring-like ledge held the fixture neatly and securely in place. In late burners this ring is not so well formed.

Both the Nutmeg and the Acorn burners take a chimney a little over an inch in diameter.

The Hornet burner resembles the Acorn in general appearance but is larger; it takes a chimney one and a half inches in diameter. These burners also take a ring for ball shades or

The three most common burners in miniature lamps are, left to right, the Acorn, The Hornet, and the Nutmeg. This illustration is from a catalog of the Plume and Atwood Manufacturing Company.

a tripod for umbrella shades. Umbrella shades are rare with the Hornet-sized burners. By far the greater number of lamps equipped with Hornet-sized burners have globe-chimney shades.

Hornet burners may be marked "P. & A. Hornet" or are plain with no marks or ornaments. One of this size was marked "Crown Improved" and was probably not made by the Plume and Atwood Company.

A foreign burner is somewhat similar to the Acorn in size and shape but is smaller, taking a chimney fifteen sixteenths of an inch in diameter. Since it is of European make it probably could properly be referred to as two and a half centimeters in size. The greater number of these are marked "Spar-Brenner," but others are marked "T & B Rukle," "Wienerbrenner Prima," "Korner & Co. Berlin," or have a pattern of diamonds and dots. The ring holder for the ball or unturned shade is usually securely attached to the upper part of the burner.

Another type of foreign burner takes a chimney one and an eighth to one and a quarter inches in diameter. Often these are the student-lamp type of chimney. It takes a globe type of shade and was probably made in Germany, for one of these lamps has "Gute Nacht" on the globe. The wick raisers are variously ornamted but we have seen none with names, legends, or dates.

The junior-sized lamps usually have burners taking a chimney one and a half inches in diameter. Many of the chimneys are of the student-lamp type. These burners take a flat wick which, beacuse of the construction of the burner, emerges through the top in the shape of a circle or ring. With foreign burners of this type the wick is inserted through a crescent-shaped opening in the bottom. With American burners the opening for inserting the wick is ⊏ shaped. We have seen one such burner equipped with two narrow wicks instead of one wider one, probably because a wide wick was not available.

The American burners are marked "The P & A M'F'G Co Victor" and "J. Dardonville, N.Y."

Foreign burners of this type are variously marked:

"Prima—Rund—Brenner"
"Super—Rund—Brenner"
"R.R.F. Paris"
An "H" surrounded by rays forming an
eight-pointed star-like pattern
A circle of stars and rays
Other complicated ornaments

The fifth type of American burner is very small and entirely different in shape from the others. It takes a tiny string wick. Some collectors call it the Sandwich burner because this is the type found on the Sandwich lamps. It was patented by Leverett H. Olmsted of Brooklyn, N.Y., on March 20, and

An advertisement from an old magazine showing the Vapo-Creso-lene vaporizing lamp in operation.

April 24, 1877. These burners take no chimney, the shade serving as both shade and chimney. There are several variants of this burner. A few are marked "P. & A. Mfg. Co.," but most are unmarked and it is not known who made them. One variant is found on the Vapo-Cresolene vaporizer.

Some dealers and collectors persist in dating a lamp from the patent date on the wick raiser of the burner if such a date is present. This is a fallacy since such hardware was manufactured for many years after the patent was issued. Furthermore, burners were often replaced so that there is no way of telling if it is the original equipment.

The amount of tarnish on a burner is a poor way to judge age unless you have had considerable experience. We have known unscrupulous people to place new burners and other lamp hardware in a chemical to tarnish them. The lamps were then sold as old.

Chimneys. Chimneys for the Nutmeg- and Acorn-sized burners come in various lengths form three and a quarter to five inches. Since chimneys are often replaced or are absent on lamps as found, some collectors either leave them off or supply their lamps with a chimney lenght that looks best. Apparently most original chimneys were made of clear glass but a few years ago reproduction chimneys in several colors made their appearance. Some frosted miniature chimneys also appeared about the same time. The cranberry Mary Gregory-type lamp had a tall cranberry chimney when found and it appears to be original. A few other lamps also have matching chimneys.

Several years ago Bob Shafer located an original box of old chimneys of an unusual type. They were for the Nutmeg-Acorn burners, three and a half inches tall with pleating extending one and a half inches down the sides from the top (*Fig.*47 book I). He generously shared some of these chimneys with us.

Most foreign burners require a fifteen-sixteenth-inch chimney that is about five and a half inches tall. These foreign lamps quite often lack chimenys and it is hard to locate replacements for them.

Chimneys for the Hornet burners also came in various lengths. Often lamps requiring the Hornet burners come with chimney-shades requiring no clear chimneys.

Some foreign lamps are equipped with the student-lamp

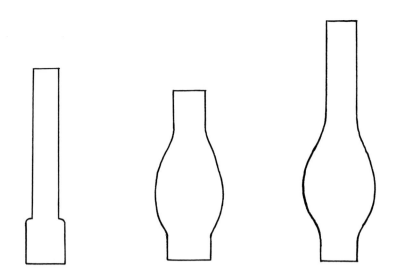

Three types of miniature lamp chimneys. *Left*: Student-lamp chimney. Some foreign lamps have this type of chimney. *Center and right*: Short and long chimneys of the type usually found on American lamps. Many foreign lamps use chimneys similar to the long type, but they are slightly smaller in diameter.

type chimney. The smaller chimneys of this type fit on burners using a round string-like wick. Many foreign lamps of the junior size use student-lamp type chimneys. These lamps are equipped with burners using flat wicks but are so constructed that the wick is rolled into a ring as it emerges from the burner.

Shades. An oil reservoir equipped with a suitable burner, wick, and chimney constitute a usable light-giving lamp. The simplest miniature lamps are nothing more. The more ornate examples were made iwth some type of shade to hide the flame, diffuse the light, and add beauty to the lamp. There are four general types of shades: the globe or ball shade; the umbrella, mushroom, or half-shade; the upturned or inverted shade; and the globe-chimney shade.

The globe shade is more or less round in shape and rests on a ring or platform attached to the burner. It requires a chimney to enclose and protect the flame.

The umbrella, also called mushroom or half shade, usually rests on a tripod attached to the burner. Sometimes a metal ring-like holder is attached to the ends of the tripod arms and in this the shade rests. In some instances the burner is equipped with two metal strips which pass up on each side of the chimney and support a metal ring about the top of the

Types of shades for miniature lamps. *Left to right*: Umbrella, Half-shade, or Mushroom type; Ball type; Globe-chimney type; and Upturned or Inverted type.

chimney. On this ring the shade hangs supported by its narrow top. In a few cases shade supported in this manner are made of cloth or wick work instead of glass. A chimney to protect the flame is used with all umbrella shades.

The upturned or inverted shade rests on a ring about the burner like that used for the globe shade. The shade flares out toward the top like an opened tulip or a bowl. The top edge of the shade may be ornamented with ruffles or an applied glass rim in contrasting color. Many of the more ornate and beautiful lamps have upturned shades. A chimney is used with these shades.

The globe-chimney shade fits inside the top of the burner in place of a separate glass chimney. Just above the burner it flares out giving room for the flame of the lamp. At the top it is constricted to form a chimney-like opening. A separate chimney is never used with this type of shade. Many of these shades are ornamented with embossed flowers or designs which causes great variation in the thickness of the glass. Since this variation in glass thickness would cause uneven distribution of the heat of the flame, this may be the reason so many of these shades are found cracked.

In colored lamps it sometimes happens that while the pattern of the base and shade match there is a slight difference in the color of the two parts. This can be explained by the two parts being made from different batches of glass. In some cases a difference in the thickness of the glass will also influence the color of the finished piece. It is probable that first-quality lamps had perfectly matching bases and shades when originally sold and discriminating collectors prefer these perfectly matched lamps today.

In painted lamps the paint, unless well fired on, is likely to be partly worn or washed off. This is particularly true of gilt which is sometimes almost entirely gone.

Some clear-glass lamps were painted to resemble either red satin or milk glass. This paint is very easily removed and such lamps are often found without a trace of paint either because it has all been removed or they had never been painted at all. The clear-glass cosmus lamp is one such example.

Other Miniature Lamps of the Kerosene Period

There are two other types of lamp coexisting with the miniature oil lamps which we will mention briefly. Both are interesting and in one group is found some of the most beautiful glass creations ever made.

Glow Lamps. This type of miniature lamp burned oil but is very different in construction from the common oil lamps (see Figs. 624 through 628 book I). The base is wide and flat and usually both base and shade are ribbed. Some shades have molded notches inside the bottom which fit into slots in the base so that a quarter turn makes them secure. Others have a metal collar into which the top shade fits.

The burner consists of a glass tube with an expanded pear-shaped bulb at the top. Into this the string-type wick fits enclosed in a spiral twisted wire which acts as a wick raiser. As the expanded bulb on the glass tube is very thin and fragile, it is often broken and the lamp is found without the glass tube and spiral wire.

There are several patterns of these lamps, all much alike. They also come in several colors: clear, red, amber, blue, green, and milk glass. Sometimes the top and bottom do not match either in color or pattern but these specimens are probably made up of the remains of two lamps. Some of the milk glass lamps are decorated with nicely painted flowers.

Fairy Lamps. The Fairy lamps were another type of small, night lamp which burned candles (*Fig.* 629 book I). They were introduced by Clark's Pyramid and Fairy Light Company of London, England, beginning about 1844.

They consisted of a variously shaped and ornamented base, a small cup for the candle, and a dome-shaped shade. The shade was often very beautifully made of the finest glass and often splendidly ornamented. Some of the shades were in the shape of castles, animals' or birds' heads, or other fantastic shapes. some of these lamps were used singly, others in beautiful and artistic clusters, Certain types are still made and sold.

Illustrations

Opium lamps old; one on left has ivory font; one on right Burmese jade. The reason for showing lamps so Collectors don't confuse them with the oil miniatures. 3-1/4" high. *Schafer collection. Photo by David J. Lans.*

Opium Lamp; nickel-plated brass with oriental design; glass shade; oriental signings under base. Commonly referred to as "Opium Smoker's Lamp". Not to be confused with the oil miniature lamps. String burner; 5-3/4" high. *McWright collection. Photo by Frank L. McWright.*

Fig. 1. Lithograph Carrying Lamp. Finished tin on gold; well worn; Oval panel on front cover contains full-figure picture of a young lady; circling the picture is a band signed "Dietz Pocket Lantern. Patd Sept. 17th, 1875". Applied handle; removable bottom font and burner; 5-3/4" high. *McWright collection. Photo by Frank L. McWright.* $260

Fig. 2. Tin lantern; applied handle; glass panels; marked on "wheel-wick raiser" patented April 25, 1861, Reis/ March 14, 1865. Unmarked burner; 8" high. *Creekman collection. Photo by Archie Johnson.* $155

Fig. 3. Brass lantern. Clear glass globe; embossed "Onion". Unmarked burner; 7" high. *Creekman collection. Photo by Archie Johnson.* $100

Fig. 4. Star Tumbler Lamp. Embossed on top of box-like lid a star and inside star "Star patented Jan. 13, 1874 Tumbler". Clear glass tumbler inverted thumbprint a round bottom, inside tin-holder rod with finger-hold-ring attached to tin font for easy removing. These tumblers were made and intended to be used by physicians or invalids for heating a little water at night. They are very rare, only a few were made because they were not practical. Font 1-1/4" high. Embossed on tumbler bottom "Taylor MFG Co. New Britain, Conn. Unmarked burner; round string-wick; 8 inches to top of handle. *Author's collection. Photo by Poist's Studio.* $275

Fig. 5. Tin Lantern; embossed on clear glass paneled globe "Perko Wonder junior". Plain font; applied handle; wick-turner signed "Perkins Marine Lamp Corp, Bkln, N.Y.". Unmarked burner; 12" high. *Stewart collection. Photo by Tom Stewart.* $80

Fig. 6. Brass Lantern; applied handle; clear glass globe secured by set screw; globe holder is hinged to allow lighting wick without removing globe; wick-turner signed "Pat. Nov. 12, 1867. Unmarked burner; 7" high. *Stewart collection. Photo by Tom Stewart.* $150

Fig. 7. Brass Lantern; applied wooden handle; font and burner assembly twist into bottom; vertical slots probably serve to frame Mica (is in glass) shield. Badger-type burner; 6-1/2" high. (not including handle) *Stewart collection. Photo by Tom Stewart.* $140

Fig. 8. No. 1. Brass Lanterns. Sometimes called "Church Going" or "Skater's Lamps." From left to right. A rope of embossing around a plain font; embossed on clear glass globe "Baby". 3/4 inches of air-vents at top of globe chimney. Finger-ring chain attached. Identical to Fig. 10. Unmarked round string-wick burner; 4-1/2" high. $475

No. 2. Plain brass font; frame and handle; embossing on top of font "Boy" Pat. Sept. 19-76; clear glass chimney; Unmarked flat-wick burner; 10-3/4 inches to top of handle. $190

No. 3. Plain brass font with applied handle; 3-1/4 inches of air-vents at top of clear glass globe chimney. Attached finger-ring chain; embossed on bottom of font "Pat-May 8, 1856. Reissued March 19, 1867." Unmarked burner round-wick; 8" high. $250

No. 4. Brass font and handle; 1-1/2 inches of air-vents at top of clear glass globe chimney. Pictured in Butler Brothers catalog "Our Drummer" April 30, 1912. No. C1226, "Klondike" Unmarked burner flat-wick; 11-3/4 inches to top of handle. $1.75 per dozen. *Authors collection. Photo by Poist's Studio.* $145

Fig. 9. Brass Lantern; emerald green globe; identical lantern shown in Butler Brothers' catalog "Our Drummer" for Apr. 1912. Referred to as NO. C1225, "The Jewel." $.79 per dozen. Globes found in blue, clear, amethyst, and amber glass. A lantern similar is also found in tin. Spots on globe reflections from camera. Unmarked burner; 7 inches high to top of lantern. *McWright collection. Photo by Frank L. McWright.* $255

Fig. 10. Brass Lantern; clear glass globe embossed "Baby." Pictured in a Dietz catalog reprint dated 1888. This lantern was purchased from a relative of the original owner who was supposed to have purchased from a relative of the original owner who was supposed to have purchased it in 1866; 1868. Unmarked burner; 4-1/2" high. *McWright collection. Photo by Frank L. McWright.* $475

Fig. 11. Brass fore-runner of the flashlight or fishing boat light. Sliding glass door; air-vent at top; two applied handles for holding with hands, attaching to belt, or securing to boat. Made by E. Miller Co. Unmarked burner; 5-3/4" high. *Creekman collection. Photo by Archie Johnson.* $130

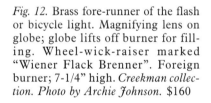

Fig. 12. Brass fore-runner of the flash or bicycle light. Magnifying lens on globe; globe lifts off burner for filling. Wheel-wick-raiser marked "Wiener Flack Brenner". Foreign burner; 7-1/4" high. *Creekman collection. Photo by Archie Johnson.* $160

Fig. 13. Brass fore-runner of the flashlight. Swinging door with magnifying glass; air-vent pushes up and down with finger-ring; stand on little platform; applied handles for holding with hands, or attaching to belt. Removable tin oil font with a pick for pulling up wick. Unmarked burner; oil font 1" high; 4 inches to top of ring. *Author's collection. Photo by Poist's Studio.* $175

Fig. 14. Jeweler's or barber's singeing lamp. Ball shape lamp with chrome plated collar and burner; small cap was used to extinguish the flame and prevent excessive evaporation of fluid; embossed on lamp "Pat. Sept. 14th. 1880, and March 14th 1893." Clear glass font comes in cobalt blue, and amber. Many collectors confuse these lamps with the oil miniatures. 5-1/4" high in upright position. *Rapai collection. Photo by Frank Lambert.* $65

Fig. 15. Jeweler's or barber's singeing lamp. Cobalt blue glass; pewter holder; embossed on top of font "Pat Sept. 14th 1880, and March 14th 1893. Not to be confused with the oil miniatures. 5 inches from bottom to top of extinguisher. *Robinson collection. Photo by Bon Graphics.* $70

Fig. 16. Cobalt blue glass; embossed on bottom of base "Pat. June 26, 1883." Probably a Jeweler's or Barber's singeing lamp with burner added, and without metal holder. Acorn burner; 3-1/4" high. *Miller collection. Aurora Photo.* $50

Opposite page bottom: *Fig. 17.* Aladdin lamp early. Also called "Cigar Lighters." Brass plated, cast metal; heavily embossed design; complete with 3-lighters across center; center for filling; flame extinguisher attached. See *Fig.* 75 in book I. Round string-wick; 3-1/4" high in center. *Author's collection.* $175

Fig. 18. Aladdin lamp. Cast metal, brass-plated; heavily embossed design. No lighters across center; center for filling. Green cased glass shade. Spot on shade reflection from camera. Not original. Acorn burner; 6-1/4" high. *Oswald collection. Photo by Cliff's Studio.* $125

Fig. 19. Aladdin brass lamp with opalescent vaseline shade; brass flame finial on stopper. U.S.A. E. Miller burner; 7-1/2" high. *Rosenberger collection. Photo by David B. Grim.* $485

Fig. 20. Aladdin lamp. Brass-plated; heavily embossed design; blue glass swirl pattern shade; marked on wickraiser "Pat. Feb. 27, 1877" Nutmeg burner; 7" high. *Caskey collection. By Ramsdell's Photo.* $270

Fig. 21. Aladdin lamp. Crystal said to be sandwich; applied handle. See *Fig. 75* in book I. Embossed ribbed shade clear glass. See Fig. 52 in book I. **Note**, shade is half an inch larger at bottom than matchholder shade. Hornet burner; 8-1/2" high. *Willis collection. Photo by Cruz Montoya.* $590

Fig. 22. Cigar-lighter lamp in cast lead. Figure of a child sitting on a pile of logs with her arm around a dog and two puppies in her lap. Holders on each side for holding lighters, but lighters missing. Blue glass ball shade. Spots on shade are reflections from camera. These lamps are sometimes not recognized as cigar-lighters. On burner "Pat. June 23, 1863." 8-1/2" high. *Author's collection.* $250

Opposite page bottom left: Fig. 23. Cigar lamp. Black metal base; embossed brass pedestal with plain brass lighters and fancy tops; font milk glass embossed basket-weave pattern around top; decorated with fired on flowers in pink and blue. Blue glass shade in thumbprint pattern. Removable brass font. Shades optional with pet ratchet burners; hornet burners can be substituted. Pet ratchet burner; 10-3/4" high. *Kerns collection. Photo by Wayne Shade.* $365

Fig. 24. Cigar lighter lamp. Bronze owl base, green glass font with red threading. Unmarked burner; round string wick. 7-1/2" high. *Wehle collection.* $385

Fig. 25. Cranberry glass. Embossed pattern; embossed "Berger Lamp" Drop-in-wick holder; pewter snuffer. 5-1/4" high. *Miller collection. Aurora Photo.* $125

Fig. 26. Herringbone ribbed lamp. Color of blue ink; applied handle. Burner is a rounded tin cap fitted onto a cork; 3-1/8" high. *Feltner collection. Photo by David B. Grim.* $125

Fig. 27. Brass base with embossed owls on a limb; font iridescent glass in a slightly ribbed swirl. Attached flame-extinguisher. Unmarked burner; round-wick; 4-3/4" high. *Author's collection. Photo by Poist's Studio.* $275

Fig. 28. Glow lamp. Milk glass; light blue melon-ribbed with embossed design and gold trim. Similar lamp shown in Montgomery Ward & Co., in their *"Buyer's Guide."* 1901 catalog No. B1440. The Glow Night Lamp is a scientific wonder, and is invaluable for the sick room, or where a small flame is required. It does not smoke, and is positively odorless, as it is generated. Made of glass in assorted colors, with globe to match. Which takes the place of a chimney and give a much softer light. Burns kerosene, and is capable of burning a long period without re-filling. One pint will burn 200 hours. This little lamp is recommended by leading physicians, and is used in nearly all of the principal hospitals in the United States. $ .25 each. See *Fig.* 625-626-628, in book I. Glass wick holder; see Fig. 624 in book I. 5" high. *Caskey collection. By Ramsdell's Photo.* $165

Fig. 29. Glow lamp. Amber glass; embossed ribs, flowers and vines. Glass wick holder; 5" high. Read "Glow" lamp caption. Fig. 28. *Caskey collection. By Ramsdell's Photo.* $175

Fig. 30. Glow thrift. Brass hanging lamp; embossed clear glass shade. Left, shown assembled on wooden stand; Right, shown unassembled. Similar to Fig. 626-627 in book I. Made by H.G. McFaddin & Co. of New York. About 1900. Shade also found in ruby flashed melon ribs. No markings on burner. Glass string-wick burner; 3-1/8" inches to top of font; 6 inches to top of shade. *Ronat collection. Photo by Arthur A. Ronat.* $210

Fig. 31. Glow lamp. Clear glass; fine raised ribbed pattern on shade, wide ribs on base. May or may not be original. See *Fig.* 626 in book I. Glass wick-holder; 5-3/8" high. *Semprini collection. Photo by Frank L. McWright.* $155

Fig. 32. Double float lamp. Victorian. Brass-plated flower stand on a slate base; embossed clear glass cups. Oil was floated on water and wick in corks were burned on the oil. 11" high. (Sometimes confused with and called Glow lamps) *Author's collection.* $240

Fig. 33. Early kerosene bluish clear glass lamp with a globe that tightens with a quarter turn and a simple slip-on base; similar to a Glow lamp Fig. 624-625 in book I. Base has vertical ribs with tiny bubbles. Spots on shade are reflections from camera. Tin cap string-wick; unmarked burner; 4" high. *Author's collection.* $175

Opposite page bottom: Fig. 34. Lamp oil fillers. Left to right: Brass with applied copper handle. 6-1/2 inches to top of center. Copper with brass spout, and brass applied handle. 4-1/2 inches to top of center. *Author's collection. Photo by Poist's Studio.* Left, $175; Right, $185

Fig. 35. Early blown glass lamp with paneled effect ribbing on base. Plain top fits on base and locks itself in place in the same manner as a Glow lamp. Greenish color. Burner is rounded tin cap; 4-1/2" high. spots are reflections from camera. *Feltner collection. Photo by David B. Grim.* $175

Fig. 36. Early clear glass lamp. Has a self-locking top; rounded tin top burner with round wick; 4-3/4" high. *Feltner collection. Photo by David B. Grim.* $150

Fig. 37. Tin reflector lamp. Pale green glass; embossed on top of font "Little Sunbeam." Tin collar; elementary wick-raiser; 5-3/8" high. *Ellis collection. Photo by Bon Graphics.* $115

Fig. 38. Pale green glass lamp. Embossed five-pointed star in center of " The New York Safety Lamp." Tin collar; reflector and elementary wick-raiser. Tin burner; 5-7/8" high. *McWright collection. Photo by Frank L. McWright.* $150

Fig. 39. Pale green glass. Embossed on front of font "The All Night Lamp Co, NY." Round-wick. May or may not have had a reflector or elementary wick-raiser. Tin unmarked burner; 4" high. *Lemon collection. Photo by Wilmyer Studio.* $135

Fig. 40. Clear glass base; faintly decorated; embossed on bottom of base "Union" white bristol shade; (prongs bent to fit shade apparently not original shade) round string-wick burner top turns easily for filling. Olmsted type burner; 3-1/2" high. *Caskey collection. By Ramsdell's Photo.* $135

Fig. 41. Clear glass embossed with name "Little Joker." White milk glass chimney shade. Olmsted burner; 1-3/4" inches high to top of font. *Miller collection. Aurora Photo.* $145

Fig. 42. Clear glass base with embossed "Little Andy." White bristol chimney-shade. See *Fig.* 15 in book I. Olmsted burner; 2-1/4" high. *Plasterer collection. Photo by Poist's Studio.* $145

Fig. 43. Clear glass stem lamp. Embossed on bottom of base "Little Favorite." white milk glass chimney-shade. Collars that fit Olmsted burners will not fit Acorn or Nutmeg burners. Made by C.S. Raymond, New York. Olmsted burner; 7-1/4" high. *Lemon collection. Photo by Wilmyer Studio.* $210

Fig. 44. Clear glass stem lamp. Embossed on base "The Little Favorite Pat. Apl'd For." Made by C.S. Raymond, New York. Collars that fit Acorn and Nutmeg burners will not fit Olmsted burner. Acorn burner; 5" high. *Author's collection.* $175

Fig. 45. Clear glass; embossed pattern; and name "Twilight" on bottom of stem base. Embossed ribs on font. White milk glass shade. Screw-on collar. Similar to *Fig.* 19 in book I. Also see *Fig.* 100. One-piece Olmsted burner; 6" high. *McWright collection. Photo by Frank L. McWright.* $210

Fig. 46. White milk glass; embossed black-painted lettering "Night Watch" six blue-painted embossed stars and red stripes around base. Chimney-shade and burner different from Fig. 47-48. Olsmted type burner; 3-7/8" high. *Feltner collection. Photo by David B. Grim.* $175

Fig. 47. White milk glass font; left showing painted fired on raised letters "Night Watch" in black; blue lines around top and bottom of base. White milk glass chimney. Font same shape as Fig. 46, but chimney-shade and burner different. Wick-raiser marked "V.C. Co." Olmsted type burner; 1-15/16" high. *Ronat collection. Photo by Arthur A. Ronat.* $175

Fig. 48. Clear glass; one side of font has raised letters "Night Watch" the other side has raised stars; white milk glass chimney-shade. Font same as Fig. 46-47; chimney-shade and burner different. Olmsted type burner; 1-15/16" high. *Ronat collection. Photo by Arthur A. Ronat.* $165

Fig. 49. Clear glass; embossed on font "Little Banner," and dots; white milk glass chimney-shade. Made by the Plume and Atwood Company, ca. 1877. Olmsted type burner; 2" high. *Miller collection. Aurora Photo.* $100

Fig. 50. Clear glass with embossed "Advance" around middle of font; white bristol chimney-shade. Olmsted burner; 4-1/2" high. *Creekman collection. Photo by Archie Johnson.* $140

Fig. 51. Clear glass; applied handle; embossed on font "Improved Little Wonder" and stars. Acorn burner; 2-1/4" high. *Miller collection. Aurora Photo.* $125

Fig. 52. Clear glass base; embossed around font "Little Wonder." White milk glass chimney shade. See Fig. 17 in book I for shade. Olmsted burner; 4-3/4" high. *Robinson collection. Photo by Bon Graphics.* $150

Fig. 53. Firefly. Clear glass base with embossed "Firefly," on side and bottom. Iron bracket gilted gold; white bristol chimney-shade. Olmsted burner; 4-1/4 inches from bottom of base to top of shade. *Rodney collection.* $720

Fig. 54. Clear glass; embossed on font "Fire-Fly" and nine stars; White bristol chimney-shade. Olmsted burner; 3-1/2" high. *McDonald collection. Photo by Ann Gilbert McDonald.* $150

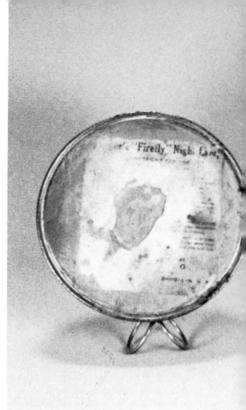

Fig. 55. Clear glass; embossed on font "Fire-Fly," collar marked pat'd. April 13, 1875 and March 21, 1876. String-type wick; unmarked burner; 2" high. *Burke collection. Photo by Archie Johnson.* $110

Fig. 56. Fire-Fly night lamp. Tin with shiny coating on top base; with milk glass beehive shade. Handle made of two rings that can be folded flat; no wick raiser, burner is adjusted by sliding up and down on tube extending up from font. The remains of a paper label glued to bottom of font. First word unreadable "Fire-Fly Night Lamp." Directions for use of kerosene only; rest of label unreadable. Manufactured in Brooklyn, NY. String wick; 2" to top of burner. *Ronat collection. Photo by Arthur A. Ronat.* $150

Fig. 57. Clear glass; embossed on font "Evening Star." Applied handle. White bristol shade. (Original) See Fig. 12 in book I. Olmsted-type burner; 2-1/2" high. McWright collection. Photo by Frank L. McWright. $150

Fig. 58. Clear glass; embossed design around bottom; embossed on font "Moon Light." White milk glass chimney-shade. Miller collection. Aurora Photo. $140

Fig. 59. Clear glass with embossed "Vienna." White milk glass chimney-shade. Collar marked "Pat'd. April 13, 1875. Olmsted burner; 2" high. Miller collection. Aurora Photo. $145

Fig. 60. Sandwich lamp. White milk glass plain pedestal base; clear glass font; white milk glass chimney-shade. See Fig. 11 in book I. Olmsted burner; 6-1/2" high. *Ford collection. Photo by Poist's Studio.* $355

Fig. 61. Pedestal base lamp. Light blue, and white milk glass; painted flowers in pink, blue, orange with green leaves; pink bands around top and bottom of shade and base. Similar to Fig. 10 in book I. Olmsted burner; 6-3/4" high. *Stewart collection. Photo by Tom Stewart.* $390

Fig. 62. Opaline glass; blue, trimmed with gold bands around base. Exactly the same color, decorations, chimney, and height as Fig. 10 in book I. White milk glass globe chimney shade. Olmsted burner; 4-5/8" high. *McWright collection. Photo by Frank L. McWright.* $260

Fig. 63. Pink opaline glass; trimmed with gold bands around base; applied handle; white milk glass globe chimney shade. See Fig. 10 in book I. Olmsted burner; 4-1/2" high. *Caskey collection. By Ramsdell's Photo.* $375

Fig. 64. Milk glass; embossed pattern on shade like Fig. 24 in book I. Embossed design on base; traces of gold remain. If not original shade-compliments base. String type burner; 5-1/2" high. *McDonald collection. Photo by Ann Gilbert McDonald.* $175

Fig. 65. Plain brass base with a row of rope embossing around top of font; white bristol chimney shade. Olmsted burner; 3-1/4" high. *Rapai collection. Photo by Frank Lambert.* $115

Top left: Fig. 66. Clear glass base; applied handle; white bristol shade. Olmsted type burner; 5" high. *Creekman collection. Photo by Archie Johnson.* $165

Above and left: Fig. 67. White bristol glass; fired on painted flowers. Red, brown, and green on one side; on right; other side of lamp has written in brown "Roton Point Conn." Olmsted-type burner; 5-1/4" high. **Note,** 1907 catalog of Burley & Tyrell Co. Chicago shows a picture of a lamp similar. "Japanese Decorated" with identical burner. *Ronat collection. Photo by Arthur A. Ronat.* $185

Fig. 68. Cobalt blue glass; applied handle; embossed on font "Wide Awake" and stars. Font clear. Acorn burner; 2-3/4" high. *Miller collection. Aurora Photo.* $160

Fig. 69. Clear glass font embossed "Little Pet." Taplin-brown collar marked with the "P" missing "ATD Apr 13 1875, and MCH 21 1886." Acorn burner; 2" high. *Cotting collection. Photo by Sisson Studio.* $125

Fig. 70. Clear glass stem lamp; embossed on font "Empire." Original pinched-in chimney; collar signed "Chinnock Pat. Sept, 5, 76" One-piece burner; 4" high. *McWright collection. Photo by Frank L. McWright.* $135

Fig. 71. Clear glass pedestal lamp embossed on font "Empire" made by Empire State Flint Glass Works. Burner dated Sept. 5, 1875. Stands 5 inches to top of burner which swivels open for filling with kerosene. *Feltner collection. Photo by David B. Grim.* $145

Fig. 72. Clear glass base; applied handle; embossed on font "Empire." No collar; extension added to Acorn burner; 4" high. *Robinson collection. Photo by bon Graphics.* $120

Fig. 73. No. 1. White milk glass lamp with poorly defined decorations of red and gold. Dated collar; Olmsted type burner; 5-3/8" high. $295
No. 2. Identically shaped butterscotch opalescent base, encircled with blue, white and orange flowers, green leaves. Dated collar; 3-1/2 inches to top of burner spout. Shade and chimney missing. *Feltner collection. Photo by David B. Grim.* $85

Fig. 74. White bristol glass; pedestal base with embossing. Foreign burner; 4-3/4" high. *Von Linden collection. Toles Photo.* $65

Fig. 75. Clear glass; embossed scroll-like design. May or may not have had a matching chimney-shade, reflector, or could be used as salt and pepper shakers. See *Fig.* 126 in book I. Acorn burner; 3" high. *Smith collection. Photo by Don Blegen.* $35

Fig 76. Milk glass; embossed floral design on front; on back, embossed small leaves and stems; paint not fired on and largely worn off; chimney new. May or may not have had a matching chimney-shade, reflector, or could be used as salt and pepper shakers. See *Fig.* 126 in book I. Acorn burner; 2-1/2" high. *Smith collection. Photo by Don Blegen.* $45

Fig. 77. Pedestal base; milk glass; painted pale yellow; embossed design trimmed in gold; paint not fired on and largely worn. Chimney new. May or may not have had a matching chimney-shade or reflector. Acorn burner; 3" high. *Smith collection. Photo by Don Blegen.* $45

Fig. 78. Melon ribbed pedestal base painted blue, mostly worn off; paint not fired on; flowers also worn. May or may not have had a matching chimney-shade or reflector. Acorn burner; 2-1/2" high. *Smith collection. Photo by Don Blegen.* $100

Fig. 79. Pedestal base; clear glass; embossed grape design; Imperial Glass Co. are making new ones and calling them "Boutique." May or may not have had a matching chimney-shade or reflector. Nutmeg burner; 3" high. *Smith collection. Photo by Don Blegen.* $35

Fig. 80. Pedestal base; clear glass; embossed six vertical beaded ribs, and one horizontal beaded rib around font. May or may not have had a matching chimney-shade, reflector, or could be used as salt and pepper shakers. See Fig. 126 in book I. Acorn burner; 3" high. *Smith collection. Photo by Don Blegen.* $35

Fig. 81. White milk glass with an embossed melon rib base; chimney simulated to look like a burnt candle. Referred to as the "Fairy" in Butler Bros. fall catalog 1905, and sold for $ .96 per dozen. Acorn burner; 6-3/4" high. *White collection. Photo by Frank L. McWright.* $125

Fig. 82. Milk glass, painted in pale yellow; paint not fired on and badly fading around top; bottom and corners embossed ribbed and painted gold. May or may not have had a matching shade, reflector, or could be used as salt and pepper shakers. See *Fig.* 126 in book I. Acorn burner; 3" high. *Smith collection. Photo by Don Blegen.* $100

Fig. I. Cameo lamp. Citron with white decorations of flowers and leaves; butterfly on back of base and shade; applied frosted feet. Possibly Stevens and Williams. English burner; 7-1/2" high. *Bartol collection. Photo by Cox Studio.* $12,600

Fig. II. Peachblow, glossy finish glass; rose shading to light; enamel gold flowers and leaves; also a gold bird on shade and a bee on base. Signed Webb. Rund-Brenner burner; 9-1/4" high. *Bartol collection. Photo by Cox Studio.* $3675

Fig. III. Stevens & Williams; mother-or-pearl satin glass in a swirled pattern; base deep rose shading to light; shade a shading yellow to green. (Original) Foreign burner; 9" high. *Schafer collection. Photo by James Hulsebus.* $3450

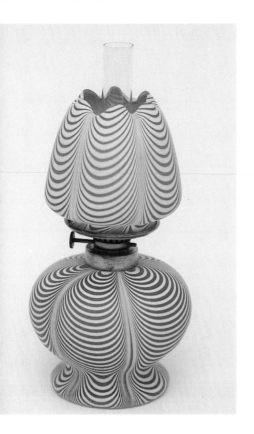

Fig. IV. Rose and white Verre Moire (Nailsea) glass, satin finish. Foreign burner; 8-1/2" high. *Cox collection. Photo by Gary Studio.* $3525

Fig. V. Peachblow; dark rose shading to light rose; applied frosted feet. Foreign burner; 8-1/4" high. *Cox collection. Photo by Gary Studio.* $3675

Fig. VI. Rainbow glass. Clear with rainbow bands of blue, pink, amber, and green. Wide bands of slightly swirled pattern. Clear glass applied shell feet. Foreign burner; 8-1/4" high. *Rodney collection.* $2650

Fig. 83. White milk glass; may or may not have had a matching chimney-shade or reflector. Acorn burner; 3-1/2" high. *Willis collection. Photo by Cruz Montoya.* $45

Fig. 84. Opalescent milk glass; embossed floral design. May or may not have had a matching chimney-shade, or reflector. Acorn burner: 3" high. *Stewart collection. Photo by Tom Stewart.* $45

Fig. 85. Opalescent milk glass; melon ribbed with embossed flowers around top and bottom of base; paint largely worn off. May or may not have had a matching chimney-shade, or reflector. Acorn burner; 3" high. *Stewart collection. Photo by Tom Stewart.* $45

Fig. 86. White milk glass; melon ribbed with embossed design. May or may not have had a chimney-shade, or reflector. Acorn burner; 3" high. *Stewart collection. Photo by Tom Stewart.* $45

Fig. 87. Diamond quilted, satin glass in chartreuse. May or may not have had a matching chimney-shade. Ca. questionable? Foreign burner; 3-1/2" high. *Duris collection. Photo by Lincoln McCabe.* $85

Fig. 88. Light blue glass; pedestal base. Acorn burner; 3-1/4" high. *Rapai collection. Photo by Frank Lambert.* $50

Fig. VII. Satin glass; embossed design; rainbow colors pink, blue, and yellow. Probably original because of colors. Kosmos Brenner burner; 10-1/2" high. *Oswald collection. Photo by Cliff's Studio.* $3780

Fig. VIII. Cased glass; pink shading to light; base rests in brass holder. Kosmos burner; 11-1/2" high. *Carman collection. Logan Photo.* $1980

Fig. IX. Satin glass; white shading to pale yellow with applied corolene decoration in pink. Applied frosted feet. Kosmos Brenner burner; 10" high. *Bartel collection. Photo by Cox Studio.* $5500

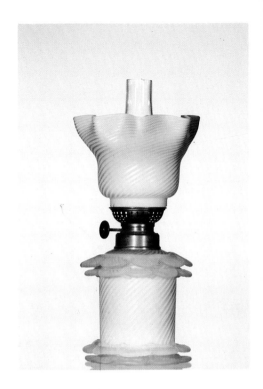

Fig. X. Blue cased glass lamp; encased in applied clear glass shell petals; petals also form skirt at base. Foreign burner; 9" high. *Hulsebus collection. Photo by James Hulsebus.* $3675

Fig. XI. Satin glass; mother-of-pearl in a ribbed swirl pattern; apricot shading to pink; applied double ruffle of frosted shell-like petals around top and bottom of base. Found in yellow shading to light. Kosmos Brenner burner; 9-1/8" high. *Rosenberger collection. Photo by David B. Grim.* $2925

Fig. XII. White satin glass; mother-of-pearl in diamond pattern; applied ribbed frosted feet; applied frosted twisted handles. Foreign burner; 12" high. *Rosenberger collection. Photo by David B. Grim.* $3850

Fig. 89. Brass saucer lamp; applied handle; blue glass font; spring to hold font securely to base. See *Fig.* 32 in book I. Nutmeg burner; wick-raiser marked 2/27/1877. 3" high. *Cashey collection. By Ramsdell's Photo.* $125

Fig. 90. Green painted tin saucer base lamp with applied brass finger-hold. Font is clear glass and screws into tin base "Pat. July 5, 1870." Collar is an early common one with two fine lines. With the advent of the Taplin Brown collar (1875-76) production of this collar ceased abruptly. Burner is very heavy brass and originally took a Flange-base chimney. Thumb screw marked "DYOTT'S Pat. Jan 6, 1868." **Note**, the very long shank on the burner. 13/16 inches long from collar to the underside of chimney ring. 2-7/8" high. *Cotting collection. Photo by Sisson Studio.* $125

Fig. 91. Tin saucer base; applied handle; clear glass embossed font "Pat. July 5, 1870. Nutmeg burner; 3" high. *Creekman collection. Photo by Archie Johnson.* $125

Fig. 92. Tin saucer base lamp; applied handle; white milk glass font; embossed ribbed swirl pattern and "Sunlight." May or may not have had a spring around bottom of font to secure to base. See *Fig.* 32 in book I. Found in pale blue glass. Hornet burner; 2-1/2" high. *Creekman collection. Photo by Archie Johnson.* $135

Fig. 93. Pedestal base lamp; light green glass; applied handle. Acorn burner; 2-7/8" high. *Duris collection. Photo by Lincoln McCabe.* $135

Fig. 94. Clear glass with embossed pattern in bottom of base; applied handle. Burner screws out of collar; top swivels and screw tightens to hold chimney. On wick raiser "Adlams Pat. Oct. 1862." 2" high. *Author's collection.* $275

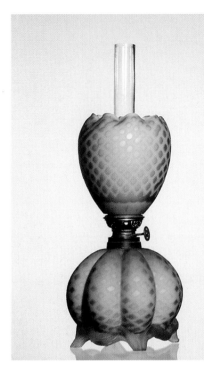

Fig. XIII. Opalescent vaseline cased glass; embossed tufted pattern. Clear vaseline glass applied feet. Foreign burner; 9-1/2" high. *Hulsebus collection. Photo by James Hulsebus.* $2600

Fig. XIV. Satin glass; raspberry; mother-of-pearl; diamond pattern; melon ribbed base with applied frosted feet. Kosmos Brenner burner; 10-1/2" high. *Rosenberger collection. Photo by David B. Grim.* $3300

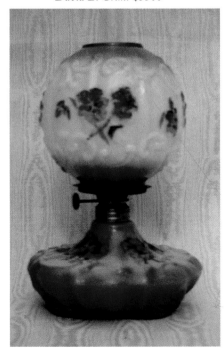

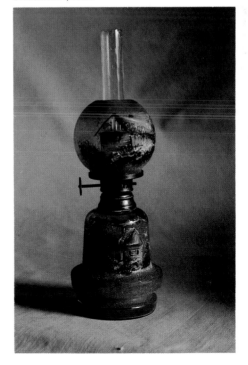

Opposite page bottom left: Fig. XV. Cased satin glass lamp; embossed ribs straight up and down in white with blue horizontal stripes; frosted applied "rigaree" shells on top and bottom of base. Foreign burner; 9-1/2" high. *Schafer collection. Photo by James Hulsebus.* $3225

Opposite page bottom right: Fig. XVa. "Spider Web" Milk glass with embossed scrolls. Painted deep pink with flowers of deep pink and orange with green leaves; Nutmeg burner; 8-1/4" high. See Fig. 292 in Book I. $385

Fig. XVI. Cranberry glass lamp with clear glass prisms; has painted-on satin finish which gives a frosted appearance. Base and shade has transparent cranberry circles outlined in enamel white dots; decorated in enamel with sprays of white flowers, and green leaves. Nutmeg burner; 8" high. *Feltner collection. Photo by David B. Grim.* $2200

Fig. XVIII. Overshot, frosted glass; house scene and surroundings in various colors. Foreign burner; 5-1/2" high. *Hulsebus collection. Photo by David J. Lans.* $1200

Fig. XVII. Three-tier pedestal base lamp; satin glass; deep pink shading to white; gold enamel decorations. Possibly Webb. Foreign burner; 9-1/2" high. *Caskey collection. Photo by Ramsdell.* $4700

Fig. 95. Clear glass; applied handle; embossed ribs on bottom of base; string type wick; embossed on wick-raiser "Gray, Boston." May or may not have had a shade. Unmarked burner; 5" high. *Ford collection. Photo by Poist's Studio.* $75

Fig. 96. Finger lamp; same pattern as *Fig.* 112 in book I. Clear glass turning to color violet with age. Embossed large bull's-eye. Applied handle. Acorn burner; 3-11/16" high. *Ronat collection. Photo by Arthur A. Ronat.* $100

Fig. 97. Clear glass balls. Supposed to be old. Spots are reflections from camera. Acorn burner; 3-1/2" high. *Bartol collection.* $75

Fig. 98. Clear glass; applied handle; embossed with fine ribbing and a design of oval beads. Found in cobalt blue and amber. Acorn burner; 3" high. *Ness collection. Photo by Poist's Studio.* $95 clear; $145 colored glass.

Fig. 99. Amber glass lamp; applied handle; embossed honeycomb pattern on inside of base. Similar to *Fig.* 38-39 in book I. Found in blue and cranberry glass. Acorn burner; 3" high. *McWright collection. Photo by Frank L. McWright.* $130

Fig. 100. Dark blue glass finger lamp; applied handle; embossed on front is a single 5 pointed star; on thumb screw of burner marked "Twilight" & "H.B. & H." Miller oval band collar. Hornet burner; 2-5/8" high. Also see *Fig.* 45. *Cotting collection. Photo by Sisson Studio.* $95

Fig. XIX. Blue glass; inverted thumb-print pattern. Enameled white, Mary Gregory type scene. Nutmeg burner; 7-1/2" high. *Hulsebus collection. Photo by James Hulsebus.* $900

Opposite page top right: Fig. XX. Opalescent glass; blue with rooster on base in varigated colors. Hen on shade has inverted paneled effect. Collar was changed for nutmeg burner; probably originally had a foreign collar and burner; Nutmeg burner; 9-1/4" high. *Feltner collection. Photo by David B. Grim.* $1200

Opposite page bottom left: Fig. XXI. Green glass with cream colored enamel decorations, and gold bands. Spots reflections from camera. Foreign burner; 5-1/4" high. *Feltner collection. Photo by David B. Grim.* $625

Opposite page bottom right: Fig. XXIa. Bull's-eye cranberry and clear glass stem lamp; 5-3/4" high; acorn burner. See Fig. 110 in Book I. $100

Fig. XXII. Overshot glass; blue shading to lighter; applied clear glass petal feet; Foreign burner; 5-3/4" high. *Rosenberger collection. Photo by David B. Grim.* $1300

Fig. XXIV. Blue glass with white opalescent daisy and fern pattern; embossed and swirled. Similar to *Fig. 290-293-294* in book I. Nutmeg burner; 6-1/2" high. *Shipman collection. Photo by Widemire Studio.* $960

Fig. XXIII. Cranberry glass; enamel decorated flowers and dots in white; trimmed in gold. Foreign burner; 6-1/4" high. *Feltner collection. Photo by David B. Grim.* $790

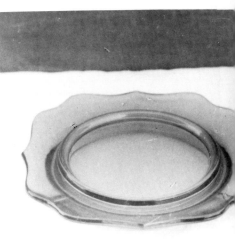

Fig. 101. Cobalt blue glass, identical in color saucer-base and nutmeg lamp. Lamp identical to other nutmeg lamps except base is slightly larger in diameter which is 3-1/16". Bottom of base is also shaped differently (see photo at left) so it will fit perfect in the depression saucer-base which measures 3-1/8". Other nutmeg lamps in various colors including the cobalt blue measure 2-15/16" which are smaller. The base and size are not identical to the other nutmeg lamps even though it may appear so to the casual observer. The chimney is new. Acorn burner; 2-1/2" high. *Smith collection. Photo by Don Blegen.* $145

Fig. 102. Novelty lamp. Clear glass in the shape of a patent medicine bottle. This could be a "One of a Kind." The bottle neck has been closed with glass; the filler neck and collar neck appear to be a part of the mold. Cork-stopped filler. Hornet burner; 6-1/4"x2-1/2"x1-1/4" high. *McWright collection. Photo by Frank L. McWright.* $175

Fig. 103. Brass saucer base with applied handle; clear glass font has notches to screw onto raised holders in the base. Printed into the base on right patented October 28th 1873 "Colar marked Patd, Apr 13, 1876-Mch 31, 1876." **Note:** wick-raiser is positioned lower than normal. Found in blue amethyst and green glass. Font identical to *Fig.* 33 in book I. Probably made by the same manufacturer. Nutmeg burner; 2-1/2" high. *Ronat collection. Photo by Arthur A. Ronat.* $75 clear; $120 colored glass.

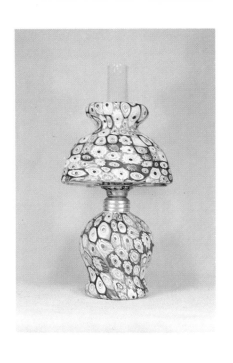

Fig. XXV. Millefiori satin glass in many colors. Believed to be old. Unmarked burner; 7-1/4" high. *Kerns collection.* $1375

Fig. XXVI. Cased glass; light green shading to white; embossed design with painted flowers. Found in blue and deep rose shading to white; pale pink shading to apricot. See *Fig.* 375 in book I. Foreign burner; 10-1/2" high. *Rodney collection.* $950

Fig. XXVII. Satin glass, burmese color decorated with rust colored leaves. Foreign burner; 6-1/2" high. *Cox collection. Photo by Gary Studio.* $1050

Fig. XXVIII. Brass pedestal base. Satin glass; mother-of-pearl in diamond pattern; blue shading to white. Burner marked H.S. (British) Foreign burner; 10" high. *Kerns collection.* $2300

Fig. XXIX. Silver pedestal base with heavily embossed wild life scene of birds, leaves, acorns and branches. Swirled embossed ribbed shade; cased glass dark rose shading to light. Foreign burner; 13-1/2" high. *Solverson collection. Photo by Van Skiver's Studio.* $880

Fig. XXX. Baccarat Rose Amber; embossed swirled design; lower half of shade frosted; "J.R. BEC ROND PARISIEN" marked on burner; Foreign burner; 9-3/4" high. *Solverson collection. Photo by Van Skiver's Studio.* $2425

Fig. 104. White milk glass on brass saucer base; orange bands at top and bottom; pink band on top; floral band with blue and yellow flowers and green leaves. Acorn burner; 3" high. *McWright collection. Photo by Frank L. McWright.* $130

Fig. 105. White milk glass decorated with blue and yellow leaves; red berries; painted red band around top of lamp; red lines around top of base; red lines around top and bottom; similar to *Fig.* 39 in book I. Acorn burner; 3" high. *Caskey collection. By Ramsdell's Photo.* $110

Fig. 106. Milk glass white; with orange band around top of lamp; red lines around top and bottom; paint fired-on blue and green floral design. Applied handle. Similar to *Fig.* 39 in book I. Nutmeg burner; 3-1/8" high. *McWright collection. Photo by Frank L. McWright.* $110

Fig. 107. Finger lamp; cranberry glass; in honeycomb pattern; applied clear glass handle; (new chimney) found in amber, clear, and blue. Acorn burner; 2-7/8" high. *Lennox collection. Photo by Barbara Swift.* $210

Fig. 108. Opaline glass; delicate blue-green; applied handle; decorated with painted white flowers and yellowish-green leaves. Nutmeg burner; 3" high. *Caskey collection. By Ramsdell's Photo.* $175

Fig. 109. Finger lamp. Green milk glass with applied handle. Fired on painted flowers in red and blue. Clear glass chimney. Foreign burner; 4" to top of burner. *Hulsebus collection. Photo by James Hulsebus.* $135

Fig. XXXI. Santa Clause. Base medium brown; light boots. Bottom of coat brown shading to yellow; light brown pack on back; face and whiskers pink; eyes not colored. Glass of shade very thin. Paint fired on uniformly but rather carelessly applied. Indentation in bottom of base. Unlike the usual Santa which is perfectly flat on bottom. Probably made by the same manufacturer. See *Fig.* VII in book I. Also found carelessly painted in brick-red with gunmetal boots. Nutmeg burner; 9-1/2" high. *Author's collection.* $4000

Fig. XXXII. Milk glass with a yellowish-cream ground; enameled multi-coloring decorations. Marked Schimdt-Jaedicke Berlin. Foreign burner; 10-1/2" high. *Carman collection. Logan Photo.* $725

Fig. XXXIII. Bristol glass; fired on ground yellowish cream; iris flowers and leaves in purple, burgundy and green; diamond and dots on wick-raiser. Foreign burner; 8" high. *Rapai collection. Photo by Frank Lambert.* $660

Fig. XXXIV. Opalescent glass; faintly green; melon-ribbed swirled pattern. Applied rope-like handle. Foreign burner; 7" high. *Rosenberger collection. Photo by David B. Grim.* $1650

Fig. XXXV. Blue glass in diamond pattern; enamel decorations in white, yellow and orange. Foreign burner; 7-1/4" high. *Feltner collection. Photo by David B. Grim.* $745

Fig. XXXVI. Pedestal base lamp; green glass. The shamrocks are painted in a satin frosted finish outlined with dots. Foreign burner; 8-1/2" high. Rosenberger burner. *Photo by David B. Grim.* $690

Fig. 110. Base, white opalescent glass with applied handle. Embossed ribbing around top and bottom; embossed flowers painted gold badly worn off. See *Fig.* 449 in book I. With shade and without handle. Hornet burner; 4-1/2" high. *Author's collection.* $135

Fig. 111. Glazed pottery base. Applied handle; grayish blue heavily embossed ribs, medallions circled in wreaths, leaves and dots. Hornet burner; 3-1/2" high. *Smith collection. Photo by Don Blegen.* $150

Fig. 112. Finger lamp. Cased glass in chartreuse shading to cream. Embossed design. Clear glass applied handle, and chimney. Foreign burner; 4" to top of burner. *Hulsebus collection. Photo by James Hulsebus.* $220

Fig. 113. Clear glass finger lamp; applied handle; embossed band of ribs around bottom of font; embossed grain and corn pattern. Embossed on base "Pat. February 11, 1873." Hornet burner; 4-1/4" high. *Solverson collection. Photo by Van Skiver's Studio.* $185

Fig. 114. Green glass lamp with applied handle; foreign chimney. Foreign burner; 3-3/4" high. *Feltner collection. Photo by David B. Grim.* $125

Fig. 115. Clear glass base; fluted pattern; applied handle. Nutmeg burner; 2-1/2" high. *Creekman collection. Photo by Archie Johnson.* $85

Fig. XXXVII. Satin glass; shading from rose to pale pink; embossed swirled ribbing with flowers, leaves and berries. Kosmos Brenner burner; 12" high. *Rosenberger collection. Photo by David B. Grim.* $1900

Fig. XXXVIII. Blue milk glass decorated with green and white birch trees, and orange mushrooms. Similar to *Fig.* 359 in book I. Foreign burner; 9-3/8" high. *Semprini collection. Photo by Frank L. McWright.* $660

Fig. XXXIX. White milk glass; fired on painted scenes in shades of blue; windmills and boats; applied clear glass ruffled feet. See *Fig.* 332 in book I. Nutmeg burner; 8-1/4" high. *Semprini collection. Photo by Frank L. McWright.* $560

Fig. XL. End-of-day glass in green and ruby; embossed swirled pattern graduating diamond shape dots trailing through middle of every other swirl; round dots between alternating swirls. Found in cranberry glass. Hornet burner; 9-1/2" high. *Semprini collection. Photo by Frank L. McWright.* $660

Fig. XLII. Opalescent glass; yellow with inverted paneling. Hornet burner; 8-1/2" high. *Rosenberger collection. Photo by David B. Grim.* $660

Fig. XLI. Amber glass; embossed medallion and rib pattern. Foreign burner; 8-3/4" high. *Semprini collection. Photo by Frank L. McWright.* $715

Fig. XLIII. Amber glass; ribbed swirled pattern; very light and delicate. Foreign burner; 7-1/4" high. *Feltner collection. Photo by David B. Grim.* $600

Fig. 116. Clear glass lamp with applied handle and fine vertical ribbing; flared-bottom chimney. "Holmes, Booth & Haydyn: burner; 2-3/8" high. *McWright collection. Photo by Frank L. McWright.* $110

Fig. 117. Hand lamp; white opalescent glass with blue "eyes." Applied blue glass handle. Hornet burner; 3" high. *Caskey collection. By Ramsdell's Photo.* $475

Fig. 118. Hand lamp; cranberry opalescent glass in hobnail pattern; clear glass applied handle. Hornet burner; 3-1/4" high. *Stewart collection. Photo by Tom Stewart.* $360

Fig. 119. Hand lamp. Embossed ribbed swirled in bands of rainbow colors pink, blue, and yellow. Applied handle. P. & A. Victor burner; 3-7/8" high. *Oswald collection. Photo by Cliff's Studio.* $470

Fig. 120. Clear glass lamp with embossed face and wig. Applied handle. Top right, showing wig; bottom right, showing face. Made by Atterbury 7 Co. Pittsburgh, Pa. On bottom of base embossed "June 10, 1868." Hornet burner; 3-3/4" high. *Battersby collection.* $715

Fig. XLIV. Blue cased glass lamp; ornamented with pink, red and butterscotch "Frosting" spattering over white. Similar to *Fig.* 516. Spar Brenner burner; 9" high. *Rosenberger collection. Photo by David B. Grim.* $825

Fig. XLV. Cranberry opalescent gold spatter glass; wide convex ribbing, and knobbed bands. Paris burner; 11-3/4" high. *Rosenberger collection. Photo by David B. Grim.* $1375

Fig. XLVI. Cased glass lamp; dark red with gold decorations well worn. Base diamond shape with embossed swirled ribs; vertical ribs with fan-shaped fronds circling the bottom of shade. See *Fig.* 541-542 in book I. Nutmeg burner; 8-1/2" high. *McWright collection. Photo by Frank L. McWright.* $1525

Fig. XLVII. Porcelain; blue with embossed design. Foreign burner; 7" high. *Rosenberger collection. Photo by David B. Grim.* $395

Fig. XLIX. Milk glass, pink melon swirl stripes; embossed decorations in brick-red. Foreign burner; 8-1/4" high. *Rosenberger collection. Photo by David B. Grim.* $625

Fig. XLVIII. Satin glass; white embossed fine melon ribbing with embossed oak leaves pale aqua trim on leaves; orange and black trim bands. Hornet burner; 7-3/4" high. *Semprini collection. Photo by Frank L. McWright.* $775

Fig. L. Satin glass; shading from deep rose to pale pink; embossed ribbing and leaves. (Original) Spar Brenner burner; 8-1/2" high. *Rosenberger collection. Photo by David B. Grim.* $1700

Fig. 121. Pirate lamp. Black glass, paint not fired on. Face embossed, flesh color, eyes blue, lips and cap on head red, eyebrow and patch on eye black. Hornet burner; 4" high. *Author's collection.* $625

Fig. 122. Heavy brass lamp; appears to be a ship's table lamp. Four very small brass studs protrude out from the collar which indicates it could have been hung by a chain, cord or wire. It has a Queen Anne burner with a gasket on the threads where it screws into the brass font. Thumb screw is marked "Made in America." A Hornet burner will fit the font. 2" to top of collar and 4-1/2" diameter at widest point. *Cotting collection. Photo by Sisson Studio.* $40

Fig. 123. Silverplated lamp with applied handle; three applied feet; embossed flowers and scrolling. Acorn burner; 2-1/2" high. *Rosenberger collection. Photo by David B. Grim.* $150

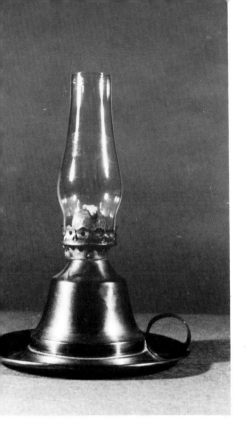

Fig. 124. Brass saucer lamp; applied embossed handle; pictured in Plume and Atwood Mfg Co. catalog, called "Cottage." Acorn burner; 2" high. *Stewart collection. Photo by Tom Stewart.* $50

Fig. 125. Brass saucer lamp; applied fancy embossed handle; has a coronet burner with flange-base chimney. thumb screw marked "E. Miller & Co" and "Meriden Conn." Similar to one shown in Plume & Atwood catalog, called "Cottage." Coronet burner; 2-1/2" high. *Cotting collection. Photo by Sisson Studio.* $50

Fig. 126. Brass finger lamp; tin bottom in font; embossed design "Bedroom Night" on applied handle. Hornet burner marked "P & A Hornet." 2" high. *Ronat collection. Photo by Arthur A. Ronat.* $40

Fig. 127. Brass finger lamp. Referred to as the "No 739 Hornet" in the P. & A. catalog; ca, 1906. Hornet burner; 2-3/8" high. *McWright collection. Photo by Frank L. McWright.* $40

Fig. 128. Brass finger lamp with embossed floral handle. Hornet burner; 1-1/2" high. *Creekman collection. Photo by Archie Johnson.* $40

Fig. 129. Brass nickel plated lamp; embossed on bottom "No. 41, Made in U.S.A." Acorn burner; 1-1/2" high. *Author's collection.* $45

Fig. 130. Brass saucer finger lamp; applied handle; marked on wheel-wick-raiser "Good Night" Pat June 1, '69." Acorn burner; 2-1/4" high. *Berryman collection. Photo by Bon Graphics.* $75

Fig. 131. Tin finger lamp; flashed red; embossed "Sterling" on side; applied handle; lamp similar to one shown in Butler Brothers catalog, called "Our Drummer" April 30, 1912, metal lacquered; assorted colors. Hornet burner; 1-3/4" high. *McWright collection. Photo by Frank L. McWright.* $40

Fig. 132. Brass finger lamp; embossed ribbing around base; applied handle. Referred to as the "No. 2127 Acorn" in the P & A catalog; ca 1906. Acorn burner; 1-3/8" high. *McWright collection. Photo by Frank L. McWright.* $40

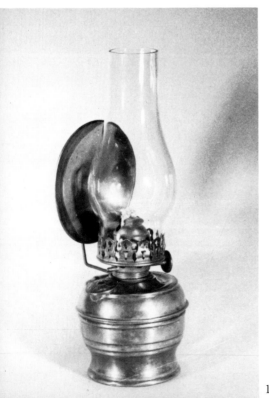

Fig. 133. Brass finger lamp; embossed ribbing around base; applied handle. Referred to as the "No. 2127. Acorn" in the P & A catalog; ca. 1906. Acorn burner; 1-1/2" high. *Creekman collection. Photo by Archie Johnson.* $40

Fig. 134. Hanging or free-standing lamp. Brass; nickel-plated reflector; on top of font embossed "Climax Reflector Nigh Lamp." Nutmeg burner; 5-1/2" high. *McWright collection. Photo by Frank L. McWright.* $75

Fig 135. "Acme" brass reflector night lamp; rod for hanging lamp missing. Right, showing pattern on filler cap; on top of font marked "All Night." Made in United States of America; some letters large and some small. Made by Edward Miller & Co. Meriden, Conn. Similar to *Fig.* 64 in book I. Hornet burner marked; "Improved Crown." 2-1/2" to top of collar and 2-7/8" diameter of reflector. *Ronat collection. Photo by Arthur A. Ronat.* $75

Fig. 136. Hanging or standing lamp. Brass; nickel-plated reflector on top of font; embossed "Climax Reflector Night Lamp." Nutmeg burner; 5-1/2" high. *Creekman collection. Photo by Archie Johnson.* $75

Fig. 137. Brass reflector lamp; embossed ribs around top of font; also on reflector; attached hanging rod; pictured in Plume and Atwood Mfg. Co. catalog called "Fireside" No. 2130. Acorn burner; 5" high. *Stewart collection. Photo by Tom Stewart.* $65

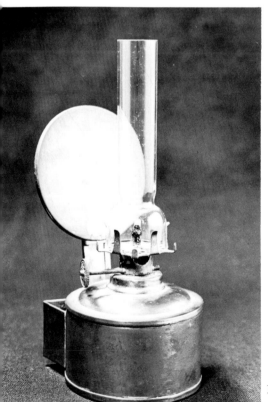

Fig. 138. Brass-plated; heavily embossed design; applied handles; similar to *Fig.* 67 in book I. Hornet burner; 3-3/4" high. *Stewart collection. Photo by Tom Stewart.* $100

Fig. 139. Very small lamp; nickel-plated base; applied handle; original chimney; marked "Luna." Olmsted type burner; 1" high. *Miller collection. Aurora Photo.* $50

Fig. 140. Brass plated hanging or standing lamp; plain reflector. Shade missing. Foreign burner; 5-1/2" high. *Robinson collection. Photo by Bon Graphics.* $60

Fig. 141. Finger lamp; brass with reflector; glass removable drop-in font. Vienna burner; 4-1/2" high. *McWright collection. Photo by Frank L. McWright.* $75

Fig. 142. Hanging reflector lamp; white milk glass font; embossed and cut-out design tin bracket. May or may not be old. Foreign burner; 3-1/2" high; 9-3/4" to top of reflector. *Stewart collection. Photo by Tom Stewart.* $85

Fig. 143. Brass base plain; embossed row of roping with a wide band of cut-out design around bottom. Hornet burner; 4-1/2" high. *Stewart collection. Photo by Tom Stewart.* $65

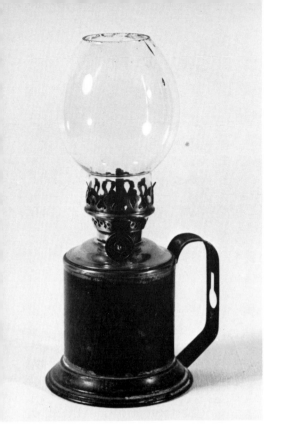

Fig. 144. Tin and brass combination; applied handle; can also be hung by handle; clear glass chimney. Foreign burner; 3" high. *Creekman collection. Photo by Archie Johnson.* $40

Fig. 145. Saucer base lamp; nickel-plated brass; applied handle; embossed "Little Queen" on top of font. Center draft burner; 5" high. *White collection. Photo by Frank L. McWright.* $150

Fig. 146. Jr. Lamp; brass-plated; heavily embossed pattern with applied embossed floral handle; made by the P & A Company and referred to as the "Little Royal Hand Lamp." Shade missing. Unmarked burner; 4-1/2" high. *Creekman collection. Photo by Archie Johnson.* $155

Fig. 147. Hanging lamp. Brass "Gimbal" mounts on wall or post (similar to those used on ships or railway cars) and remains level when mounted in any direction. Acorn burner; 4-1/2" high. *Creekman collection. Photo by Archie Johnson.* $140

Fig. 148. Brass pedestal base; similar to *Fig.* 102 in book I. Original shade broken. Spar-Brenner burner; 3-1/4" high. *Stewart collection. Photo by Tom Stewart.* $85

Fig. 149. Three-tier base; pedestal and lower font brass; upper font copper. Foreign burner; 2-3/4" high. *Duris collection. Photo by Lincoln McCabe.* $50

Fig. 150. Tin pedestal base lamp with embossed ribbing around bottom; Gild-painted. Found painted dark green, blue and maroon. Identical lamp shown in a Juno catalog reprint on page 78 of Freeman's "New Light On Old Lamps." Acorn burner; 5" high. *Feltner collection. Photo by David B. Grim.* $55

Fig. 151. Heavy brass pedestal lamp; white bristol shade. Similar to *Fig. 73* in book I. Foreign burner; 8" high. *Cotting collection. Photo by Sisson Studio.* $75

Fig. 152. Nickel-plated, cast metal, fluid-type lamp. White milk glass shade. Signed "Tito Landi, Made in Paris France Repose" under pedestal base. Ca. of lamp is questionable. Drop-in burner; 5-1/4" high. *McWright collection. Photo by Frank L. McWright.* $75

Fig. 153. Copper peg lamp. Saucer candle-holder; applied handle; removable plain clear glass font; font 2" high. Hornet burner; 10" high. *Smith collection. Photo by Don Blegen.* $165

Fig. 154. Brass stem saucer lamp; hammered effect design inside saucer base. Acorn burner; 4-1/2" high. *McWright collection. Photo by Frank L. McWright.* $75

Fig. 155. Brass stem saucer lamp; hammered effect design inside saucer base; cobalt blue glass in melon ribbed swirl design. Nutmeg burner; 4-1/2" high. *Stewart collection. Photo by Tom Stewart.* $135

Fig. 156. Amber glass; font similar to Fig. 116 in book I. But with raised diamonds and not fishscale. Brass saucer base same as *Fig. 157*. Stamped in collar "Patd, Apr 13, 18—Mch 31, 1876." 4-3/8" high. Also comes in clear glass and cobalt. *Ronat collection. Photo by Arthur A. Ronat.* $125

Fig. 157. Amber glass embossed design in font; brass stem, saucer shaped base lamp. Stamped in brass collar "patd Apr, 13, 1875-Mch, 31, 1876." Base same as *Fig. 156*. Found in blue and clear glass. Acorn burner; 4-3/8" high. *Ronat collection. Photo by Arthur A. Ronat.* $125

Fig. 158. Brass base with removable brass font; milk glass decorated with butterflies, leaves, and vines in the Delft manner; shade missing; embossed on wick-raiser "Pat Feb, 27. 189?." Hornet burner; 5" high. *Creekman collection. Photo by Archie Johnson.* $110

Fig. 159. Clear glass stem lamp; embossed pattern; frosted font with embossed ferns and flowers. Acorn burner; 5-1/2" high. *Reith collection. Photo by Michael Clifton.* $155

Fig. 160. Clear glass stem base; embossed design on base; embossed floral design on frosted glass font; paint not fired-on and largely worn off. Acorn burner; 5-1/4" high. *Berryman collection. Photo by Bon Graphics.* $140

Fig. 161. Stem lamp. Clear glass turning to violet color from age. Embossed "Prism" pattern. Hornet size burner marked "Improved Crown." 6-1/2" high. Made by Atterbury & Co. of Pittsburgh, Pa. *Ronat collection. Photo by Arthur A. Ronat.* $125

Fig. 162. Stem base; clear glass with embossed design inside the stem. Similar to *Fig.* 161. Acorn burner; 5-3/8" high. *Ronat collection. Photo by Arthur A. Ronat.* $65

Fig. 163. Stem base lamp; clear glass embossed ribbing inside the stem; pictured in C.M. Livingston's Silent Salesman catalog, Jan, 1894 called "Dime Leader." $ .96 per dozen. pattern in stem and collar different from *Fig.* 162. Notice difference in chimney around top has six dips or grooves for ladies to hold the curling iron steady while heating to curl their hair. Acorn burner; 5" high. *Smith collection. Photo by Don Blegen.* $65

Fig. 164. Pedestal stem lamp; clear glass; embossed ribs on the top and bottom of font separated by a plain band; swirled ribs on the stem and underside of the base. Acorn burner; 6-5/8" high. *White collection. Photo by Frank L. McWright.* $120

Fig. 165. Pedestal stem lamp; clear glass; fine rib pattern embossed on the inside of the font and the underside of the base. Acorn burner; 6-1/4" high. *White collection. Photo by Frank L. McWright.* $120

Fig. 166. Excellent quality glass, hexagon stem lamp; pattern on inside of outside smooth font; stem base pattern inside, smooth on top. Acorn burner marked "The P & A Mfg. Co. Acorn 5-5/8" high. *Ronat collection. Photo by Arthur A. Ronat.* $120

Fig. 167. Clear glass; stem base; embossed vertical ribs "Ice-Cycle" pattern. Hornet burner; 6" high. *Berryman collection. Photo by Bon Graphics.* $120

Fig. 168. Clear glass pedestal base with clear glass inverted hobnail, and embossed clear glass diamond pattern font. Acorn burner; 5-1/2" high. *Stewart collection. Photo by Tom Stewart.* $120

Fig. 169. Clear glass stem with round base; top of font clear; surrounding font embossed small diamonds and ribbon design forming a tulip pattern. Metal collar dated but not clear "Pat'd April 13, 07," Acorn burner; 4-1/2" high. *Rapai collection. Photo by Frank Lambert.* $120

Fig. 170. Clear glass stem lamp. Fishscale with cable pattern font. Made by Dalzell, Gilmore and Leigton. Findlay Ohio. Acorn burner; 5-1/4" high. *McWright collection. Photo by Frank L. McWright.* $120

Fig. 171. Clear glass lamp; octagon font; raised design on stem base. Acorn burner, marked "The P & A Mfg. Co. Acorn." 5-1/4" high. *Ronat collection. Photo by Arthur A. Ronat.* $90

Fig. 172. Clear glass font with embossed design stem lamp; base is the same as in *Fig.* 115 in book I, but font is clear with no design or frosting. Acorn burner; marked "The P & A Mfg. Co. Acorn. 5-1/4" high. *Ronat collection. Photo by Arthur A. Ronat.* $90

Fig. 173. Pedestal stem lamp; clear glass; beehive patterned font; embossed ribs on underside of base. Holmes, Booth and Haydyn burner; 5-1/4" high. *White collection. Photo by Frank L. McWright.* $80

Fig. 174. Stem base; clear glass with embossed medallions inside the base. Medallions different than *Fig. 178.* Acorn burner; 5" high. *Smith collection. Photo by Don Blegen.* $80

Fig. 175. Stem base; clear glass. Acorn burner; 5" high. *Smith collection. Photo by Don Blegen.* $70

Fig. 176. Clear glass stem lamp; on top of glass collar printed "Patented 1911," unable to read rest of date; brass insert in glass collar. Acorn burner-marked "The P & A Mfg. Co. Acorn." 5-3/8" high. *Ronat collection. Photo by Arthur A. Ronat.* $70

Fig. 177. Clear glass stem lamp. Acorn burner marked "The P & A Mfg. Co. Acorn." 5" high. *Ronat collection. Photo by Arthur A. Ronat.* $60

Fig. 178. Stem base lamp; clear glass stem and font with embossed medallions inside the base. Acorn burner; 5" high. *Smith collection. Photo by Don Blegen.* $65

Fig. 179. Clear glass stem lamp with a swirl pattern; pattern same but unlike Fig. 475 in book I. Brass insert in glass collar; on top collar "Patented Sep. 19 & Nov. 14, 1911." In C.M. Livingston's Silent Salesman catalog January 1894, it shows a picture of the lamp called "Dime Leader." $.96 per dozen. Acorn burner; 4-7/8" to top of font; 5-1/8" to top of collar. *Ronat collection. Photo by Arthur A. Ronat.* $65

Fig. 180. Frosted glass stem lamp; Bull's-eye pattern; paint fired on roses in red, yellow and green leaves. See *Fig.* 110 in book I. Acorn burner; 9-1/2" high. *Stewart collection. Photo by Tom Stewart.* $100

Fig. 181. Stem base lamp; blue glass with embossed pattern around font. Chimney and shade missing. On burner dated March 1893. Foreign burner; 8" high. *Willis collection. Photo by Cruz Montoya.* $120

Fig. 182. Clear glass base with hobnail and vertical ribbing; light blue hobnail globe chimney shade; paint probably worn off base; found in frosted glass and other painted colors; paint not fired on. These lamps were filled with perfumed oil and sold in the late 1940s and 1950s. Acorn burner; 7" high. *Stewart collection. Photo by Tom Stewart.* $25

Fig. 183. Clear glass; swirled pattern. These lamps were filled with perfume oil and sold in the 1920s and 1930s. See *Fig.* 119 in book I. Screw-on collar. Acorn burner; 7-1/2" high. *Creekman collection. Photo by Archie Johnson.* $25

Fig. 184. Left to right: Clear glass painted on inside; paint soon washes off. Embossed ribbed swirl on top with a band of embossed lines around bottom of base. Brass embossed reflector and a swirl embossed clear glass chimney. Tin handle. Nutmeg burner; screw-on top; 2-1/4" high. Identical to lamp on left; clear glass without reflector. These lamps about 1940s, 1950s. *Ness collection. Photo by Poist's Studio.* $25

Fig. 185. Left: Embossed ribbed swirl, clear glass chimney. Right: Clear glass; embossed design; clear glass chimney. No wick-turners. (Not Old) Probably in the late 1950s or 1960s. Perhaps later. Screw-on top; foreign burner; 2-1/4" high. *Ness collection. Photo by Poist's Studio.* $15

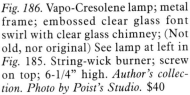

Fig. 186. Vapo-Cresolene lamp; metal frame; embossed clear glass font swirl with clear glass chimney; (Not old, nor original) See lamp at left in *Fig.* 185. String-wick burner; screw on top; 6-1/4" high. *Author's collection. Photo by Poist's Studio.* $40

Fig. 187. Clear glass; embossed fine ribbed pattern; shade signed "Holophane" at top edge. If not original the combination looks nice together. Base could be used as salt and pepper shaker, see *Fig.* 126 in book I. Ca. questionable. Acorn burner; 5-1/4" high. *Semprini collection. Photo by Frank L. McWright.* $35

Fig. 188. The latest novelty. "Little Puck" lamp is the smallest complete lamp in existence, only 4" tall to top of chimney. Has a polished nickeled base; clear glass font with horizontal ribbing and a pleated paper shade. It is practical, useful and ornamental. A perfect miniature lamp—A harmless pleasing toy. A very acceptable present for either girl or boy. On other side of the box it reads. The little "Puck" lamp can be either choice, a perfume bottle, night lamp, and toy combined. It is perfectly harmless, non-explosive, one-candle power. Burns either lard-oil or coal-oil (kerosene). Complete in every detail, perfect in design, finish and style. Will burn 10 hours without refilling. Manufactured only by McCormick & Co. Perfumers Baltimore, Md. U.S.A. Extra chimney and shades can be had for the "Little Puck Lamp" price each $.05 in a mailing carton, either from your dealer or McCormick & Co. Unmarked burner. **Note,** Apparently old, for kerosene to be called coal-oil in ad. Years ago it was always referred to as coal-oil instead of kerosene. *Smith collection. Photo by Don Blegen.* $45

Fig. 189. Milk glass base with embossed ribs and swirl design; decorated with painted blue and orange flowers; embossed ribbed shade; if shade isn't original it does compliment the base. Acorn burner; 6" high. *Creekman collection. Photo by Archie Johnson.* $35

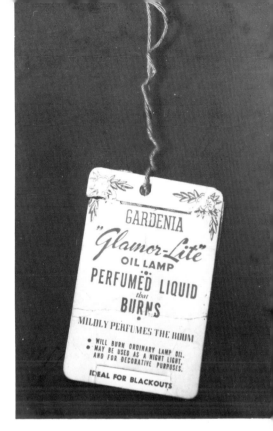

Fig. 190. White satin glass smooth font with painted, not fired-on flower decorations in red and white. Chimney is half frosted rough, other half clear glass. Shade made of parchment-paper, background green to match cotton fringe around top and bottom. Flowers painted red and white with green leaves. Shade rests on chimney; lamp filled with perfumed oil for burning was sold in the late 1940s. See label at right that came with lamp. Acorn burner; screw-on top. 6-3/4" high. *Ness collection. Photo by Poist's Studio.* $20

Fig. 191. Dark amber glass with embossed swirls; bottom marked "Mulga" screw-on collar; ca. of lamp questionable. Foreign burner; 3-1/2" high. *Stewart collection. Photo by Tom Stewart.* $15

Fig. 192. Cobalt blue glass; applied handle; wick-riser marked "Jowa made in Denmark." Ca of lamp questionable. Spots are reflections from camera. Foreign burner; 7-1/2" high. *Stewart collection. Photo by Tom Stewart.* $125

Fig. 193. Cobalt blue glass; applied handles; frosted swirl shade. Shade and base original; ca. of lamp questionable. Foreign burner; 7-3/4" high. *Duris collection. Photo by Lincoln McCabe.* $145

Fig. 194. Pedestal base lamp; cranberry glass; enameled flowers and decorations with gold bands. Possibly had a shade. Crown A D & R Co.; flat-wick burner; 8-1/2" high. *Carman collection. Photo by Logan.* $105

Fig. 195. Left: Shade green glass finger lamp; applied handle. Shades optional. Hornet burners can be substituted for Pet Ratchet. Spots are reflections from camera. Pet Ratchet burner; 6-3/4" high. Right: Base without shade, showing Pet Ratchet burner with flame extinguisher attached. *Stewart collection. Photo by Tom Stewart.* $130 left; $75 right.

Fig. 196. Dark amber glass base with applied handle; shade dark red almost looking like amber. Shades are optional and hornet burners may be substituted. Spots on shade and base are reflections from camera. Two circles of dots on burner. Pet Ratchet burner; 7" high. *Boles collection.* $130

Fig. 197. Roman key pattern on clear glass base; round green glass globe shade; extinguisher on chain attached to burner, E. Miller Co. On wick-raiser "made in U S A." Pet Ratchet burners are interchangeable; Hornet burner can be substituted. Shades are optional. Pet Ratchet burner; 9-1/2" high. *Caskey collection. By Ramsdell's Photo.* $125

Fig. 198. Pedestal base; ruby red glass (almost looks like pigeon blood). Shades for Pet Ratchet burners are optional. Spots on shade are reflections from camera. Pet Ratchet burner; 9-1/4" high. Hornet burners can be substituted. *Ford collection. Photo by Poist's Studio.* $135

Fig. 199. Amber glass base; matching amber globe shade; embossed on base "L'ANGE GARDIEN EXTRA-C. H. BINKS & CO. MONTREAL." Pet Ratchet burners take a size Hornet burner and shades are optional. Spots are reflections from camera. Pet Ratchet burner; 7-1/4" high. *Rapai collection. Photo by Frank Lambert.* $155

124

Fig. 200. Electric blue glass; applied handle; embossed on font "L'ANGE GARDIEN EXTRA-C. H. BINKS & CO. MONTREAL." Base similar to *Fig.* 199 but apparently the collar is smaller. Nutmeg burner; 3" high. *Miller collection. Aurora Photo.* $95

Fig. 201. Brass finger lamp with optional pink cased glass shade. Referred to as the "No. 342 Planters" hand lamp in the P & A catalog, ca. 1906. A later version of the lamp was sold by the Dennison Manufacturing Co., and called "Sealing Wax Lamp." Spots on shade are reflections from camera. Hornet burners can be substituted for Pet Ratchet burners. Pet Ratchet burner; 6-1/4" high. *McWright collection. Photo by Frank L. McWright.* $75

Fig. 202. Brass; with embossed applied handle; tin bottom. Stamped on bottom "Made in the United States of America." No markings on burner. Extinguisher missing. Pet Ratchet burner; 3-1/4" high. *Ronat collection. Photo by Arthur A. Ronat.* $40

Fig. 203. Green glass; applied handle; round string-wick; attached flame extinguisher; shades optional; Pet Ratchet burners can be substituted for Hornets. Spots are reflections from camera. Pet Ratchet burner; 7-1/4" high. *Ford collection. Photo by Poist's Studio.* $130

Fig. 204. Blue glass; applied handle; camphor-finished shade. Found in green, amber, amethyst and clear glass with matching colored shades. Shades optional; hornet burners can be substituted for Pet Ratchet burners. Pet Ratchet burner; 7" high. *McWright collection. Photo by Frank L. McWright.* $140

Fig. 205. Cranberry glass; applied clear glass handle; diamond pattern. Shades optional; hornet burners can be substituted for Pet Ratchet Burners. Found in blue and clear glass. Pet Ratchet burner; 6" high. *Hulsebus collection. Photo by David J. Lans.* $300

Fig. 206. Clear glass base with applied crooked handle; embossed rib and oval pattern; cobalt blue globe shade; shades are optional; Hornet burners can be substituted for Pet Ratchet burners. See *Fig.* 207. Pet Ratchet burner; 6-3/4" high. *Rapai collection. Photo by Frank Lambert.* $95

Fig. 207. Clear glass base; embossed design; applied handle. Hornet burner; 2-7/8" high. *Ellis collection. Photo by Bon Graphics.* $75

Fig. 208. Finger lamp. Textured base looking like pottery in aqua and orange color. Applied branch handle in brown with applied green leaves. Clear glass shade fits over brass wick-holder. Similar to Pet Ratchet burner. Foreign burner; 8" high. *Hulsebus collection. Photo by James Hulsebus.* $275

Fig. 209. Clear glass base paneled with applied handle. Metal tripod with prongs to fit on chimney to hold shade. Hornet size burner marked "Sterling U.S.A." 7-1/2" high. *Author's collection.* $125

Fig. 210. World's Columbian Exposition clear glass lamp; font embellished with banners bearing the dates 1492 & 1892; globe of the world also bears these dates and "Chicago." Collar and chimney may or may not be original. Small burner; 7-1/2" to top of frosted chimney. *Feltner collection. Photo by David B. Grim.* $125

Fig. 211. Brass pedestal lamp with clear ovoid shade which is marked off in vertical and horizontal lines resembling the markings on a terrestrial globe. Foreign burner; 7" high. *Feltner collection. Photo by David B. Grim.* $110

Fig. 212. Embossed design base and shade; base green; shade clear with a green tint. (Original) Pull-up type wick. Spots on base are reflections from camera. *Author's collection.* $200

Fig. 213. Opalescent vaseline glass with swirl stripes; brass reflector bracket. Similar to a "Lace-Mak-er's lamp. Foreign burner; 9" high. *Ritter collection.* $275

Fig. 214. Clear green glass lamp; with a cut in pattern, and embossed beading. Found in blue and white milk glass. Spots are reflections from camera. Hornet burner; 9-1/2" high. *Author's collection.* $250

Fig. 215. Cobalt blue glass lamp. Nutmeg burner; 6-1/2" high. *Hulsebus collection. Photo by James Hulsebus.* $275

Fig. 216. Glass blown finger lamp with applied handle. Glass has greenish cast and has the general appearance of Jersey glass. Chimney not old. Olmstead type burner; 4" high. *Feltner collection. Photo by David B. Grim.* $150

Fig. 217. Amber colored glass; embossed ribbing around top of font and top of shade; decorated with pink flowers. Hornet burner; 7-1/2" high. *Cox collection. Photo by Karen & Keith Cox.* $275

Fig. 218. Twinkle lamp; green glass with embossed name "Twinkle" and stars on base and shade. Painted flowers in white with green leaves. Paint not fired on and partly worn off. See *Fig. 432 in book I.* Acorn burner; 7" high. *Boles collection.* $380

Fig. 219. Green glass lamp. Original shade embossed with band of horizontal rings at top and vertical rows of beads separating the ribs; multi-colored flowers on base, paint not fired on and badly worn. Found in blue, amethyst, and clear glass. Acorn burner; 6" high. *Smith collection. Photo by Don Blegen.* $150

Fig. 220. Blue glass; raised fluted embossing at top of chimney shade. If not original shade, compliments base. Acorn burner; 6-5/8" high. *Semprini collection. Photo by Frank L. McWright.* $150

Fig. 221. Blue glass; embossed bar and bead pattern on base; embossed bead pattern on chimney shade. Shade similar to *Fig.* 219. If shade isn't original it compliments base. Acorn burner; 6-1/2" high. *Semprini collection. Photo by Frank L. McWright.* $225

Fig. 222. Clear glass; embossed flowers and ribs; same flower as on lamp in *Fig.* 155 in book I. Acorn burner; 6-1/2" high. *Creekman collection. Photo by Archie Johnson.* $185

Fig. 223. "Duchess" lamp by Cambridge, clear glass, squatty six-paneled base with ribbing around top, faintly embossed fern and sunburst design; chimney may or may not be original but certainly lends itself well if not. Lamp not to be confused with *Fig.* 175 in book I. Acorn burner; 7" high. *Feltner collection. Photo by David B. Grim.* $125

Fig. 224. "Countless" lamp by Cambridge, clear glass, squatty base with embossed Acanthus leaf design and thumbprint design around bottom and top of base. Chimney may or may not be original. Acorn burner; 6" high. *Feltner collection. Photo by David B. Grim.* $125

Fig. 225. Bead and panel pattern; clear six-sided base with embossed beaded swag design. Chimney has ten panels, but faintness of every other rib gives it the appearance of having only five panels. Lamp like this was pictured in the Fostoria Glass catalog of 1906 and was referred to as the "No. 19 Night Lamp." Found in cobalt blue. Nutmeg burner; 7" high. *Feltner collection. Photo by David B. Grim.* $125 clear; $150 colored glass.

Fig. 226. Finger lamp; orangish amber color with matching shade; applied handle. Foreign burner; 6" high. *McWright collection. Photo by Frank L. McWright.* $225

133

Fig. 227. Turquoise glass decorated with a silver transfer of grapes and leaves. Hornet burner; 9" high. *White collection. Photo by Frank L. McWright.* $325

Fig. 228. Clear glass; embossed pedestal base with clear font. Embossed matching shade. Font identical to *Fig.* 480 in book I. Found in amber and blue. Made by McKee and Bros. Pittsburgh, Pa. Nutmeg burner; 8" high. *Reith collection. Photo by Michael Clifton.* $325 clear; $450 colored glass.

Fig. 229. Pedestal base lamp; embossed ribs and dots on base. Shade and base identical in color cobalt blue; Globe chimney-shade faintly paneled like *Fig.* 229 in book I. May or may not be original. This combination has been seen together quite frequently. Hornet burner; 9-1/2" high. *Ford collection. Photo by Poist's Studio.* $225

Fig. 230. Cranberry glass; embossed beads and ribs. Straight up and down, unlike the beaded swirls. Hornet burner; 9" high. *Terrio collection. Photo by Poist's Studio.* $550

Fig. 231. Bluish-green glass embossed with an orange-skin textured design, embossed cattails and flowers. Similar to *Fig.* 272 in book I. *Caskey collection. By Ramsdell's Photo.* $375

Fig. 232. Green glass lamp trimmed with gold and pink dots. Paint not fired on. Similar to *Fig.* 138 in book I. Hornet burner; 7" high. *Author's collection.* $270

Fig. 233. Cranberry glass; swirl pattern. Similar to *Fig.* 290-293-294, in book I. Nutmeg burner; 6" high. *Caskey collection. Ramsdell's Photo.* $450

Fig. 234. Clear glass (believed to be flint) embossed melon ribbed swirl. Made by George Duncan and Sons of Pittsburgh, Pennsylvania. ca. 1890s. It was referred to as "Duncan's Narrow Swirl night Lamp." Nutmeg burner; silver; marked 2/27/1877. 7-1/4" high. *Caskey collection. By Ramsdell's Photo.* $335

Fig. 235. Clear glass with embossed thumb print and ribbed pattern; Applied handle. Nutmeg burner; 6" high. Mr. & Mrs. Al Newton of Red Rooster Antiques at Delanco, N.J. loaned the shade for this picture. *Author's collection.* $385

Fig. 236. Pressed pattern clear glass lamp; base and shade partly frosted. Base like Fig. 148 and 151 in book I, but the shade is different. Found in all clear glass and also blue satin. Nutmeg burner; 6" high. *Author's collection.* $325 clear and frosted; $525 blue satin.

Fig. 237. Clear glass lamp with embossed swirl pattern. Top assembled; Bottom unassembled. See Fig. 41 in book I. Acorn burner; 5" high. *Author's collection.* $500

Fig. 238. Log cabin or school house lamps. There are two sizes, small and large. Small size is 3-1/2" high, 4" wide including handle. White milk glass and blue milk glass. Large size is 3" high and 4-7/8" wide including the handle: Clear light amber, pale green, and white milk glass. Both sizes use a hornet burner. *Oswald collection. Photo by Cliff's Studio.* $350 clear; $725 colored glass.

Fig. 239. Milk glass; blue flowers on base; paint not fired on and partly worn off; shade may or may not be original. Acorn burner; 5" high. *Creekman collection. Photo by Archie Johnson.* $125

Fig. 240. Sea shells of various kinds painted in various colors; embedded in putty and covered with varnish. Probably never had a shade. Nutmeg burner; 3" high. (Believed to be old) *Author's collection.* $75

138

Fig. 241. White milk glass base; rose-petal like pattern; glass chimney-shade; traces of gilt remain on both shade and base. Similar to *Fig.* 170 in book I. Acorn burner; 5-1/8" high. *Cox collection. Photo by Karen & Keith Cox.* $135

Fig. 242. Clear glass with pressed rose design; painted red and gold; paint not fired on and sometimes partly or entirely missing. This glass is referred to as "Goofus glass." See *Fig.* 152 in book I. Clear glass chimney-shade embossed with flowers and scrolls similar to *Fig.* 154 in book I. This combination has been seen in milk glass, paint partly worn off; green and clear glass, all with the same clear glass shade in same pattern. Acorn burner: 7-1/4" high. *Smith collection. Photo by Don Blegen.* $135

Fig. 243. Another type of the Wild Rose variations, originally painted in the "Goofus" manner. Acorn burner; 6-7/8" high. *Feltner collection. Photo by David B. Grim.* $135

Fig. 244. Porcelain; embossed design in olive-green. Foreign burner; 7" high. *Von Linden collection. Toles Photo.* $330

Fig. 245. Clear glass with embossed leaf decorations. Painted in pale pink with gold decorations. Paint not fired on. Similar to *Fig. 127, 256,* and *259* in book I. Acorn burner; 8" high. *Author's collection.* $185

Fig. 246. Milk glass; embossed ribbed swirl, scroll design in burgundy and mint-green. Hornet burner; 8-1/4" high. *Lemon collection. Photo by Wilmyer Studio.* $375

Fig. 247. White milk glass lamp. Paneled with embossed leaf design; golden brown paint not fired on and partly worn off. In catalog listed the lamp as "Dixie" made by Fostoria. Hornet burner; 8" high. *Author's collection.* $300

Fig. 248. Milk glass; embossed ribbed chimney-shade; embossed design on base; blue flowers; green leaves trimmed in gold; paint not fired-on and largely worn; base similar to *Fig.* 257 in book I, without the embossing. May or may not be original, but paint on shade matches base. Hornet burner; 7" high. *Kerns collection. Photo by Poist's Studio.* $260

Fig. 249. Blue milk glass with embossed design. Also comes in white, green and pink. Hornet burner; 9" high. *Schafer collection. Photo by David J. Lans.* $350 white milk glass; $450 colored glass.

Fig. 250. Milk glass lamp; embossed bows, torches and wreaths; painted green. Globe chimney shade. Hornet burner; 8" high. *Stewart collection. Photo by Tom Stewart.* $280

Fig. 251. Pedestal base; milk glass with some flashed on color-pink, badly worn; embossed globe chimney shade like *Fig. 183* in book I, but flowers different; pink flowers with green leaves matches this base like *Fig. 152* in book I, and shade. This combination has been seen several times and believed to be original. Hornet burner; 9-1/2" high. *Ford collection. Photo by Poist's Studio.* $165

Fig. 252. Milk glass with fired-on paint to resemble satin glass in white with pink shadings; vines in brown and pink; instead of a metal tripod, there is a round clear glass shade-holder which fits into the burner and holds the umbrella-type shade. Base and shade signed "Harrison 1892" Dithridge referred to this lamp as the "Baby Cleveland." Similar to *Fig.* 218 in book I. Hornet burner; 9-1/4" high. *McWright collection. Photo by Frank L. McWright.* $735

Fig. 253. Milk glass; green with embossed design. Found in blue. Acorn burner; 5-1/4" high. *Author's collection.* $330

Fig. 254. Yellow cased glass; embossed ribbed swirl with four recessed medallions in shade and base; applied clear glass stubby feet. Found in various colors, and also End-Of-Day, overshot and crackle glass. Nutmeg burner; 8-3/8" high. *Cotting collection. Photo by Sisson Studio.* $1475

Fig. 255. White luster finish glass; embossed design; trimmed in gold, paint not fired-on and largely worn off. Clear glass prisms. Lamp old, perfect match in base and shade but doesn't show in picture. Similar to *Fig. 419* in book I. Nutmeg burner; 7" high. *Oswald collection. Photo by Cliff's Studio.* $550

Fig. 256. Milk glass lamp; light green with embossed design. Pattern called "Primrose." Found in blue and white. Made by Gillinder and Sons, Philadelphia, Pa. ca. 1896. Nutmeg burner; 7" high. *Ford collection.* $440 white milk glass; $575 colored glass.

Fig. 257. Milk glass lamp with embossed scrolling, dots, red iris, and green leaves. This pattern was known as "Wild Iris" night lamp. Made by Consolidated Lamp and Glass Co., ca. 1889. Nutmeg burner; 8-1/4" high. *Author's collection.* $350

Fig. 258. Milk glass lamp; painted pale pink and blue ground coloring, with gold highlights all badly worn. Embossed pattern. Similar to *Fig.* 243-250 in book I. Many variations of this lamp are known and are referred to as the "Family Group." Made by same manufacturer. Nutmeg burner; 7" high. *McWright collection. Photo by Frank L. McWright.* $325

Fig. 259. Milk glass; painted blue; embossed ribbing, flowers and leaves; paint not fired on and badly fading. Unlike shade in *Fig.* 135 in book I. Hornet burner; 7-1/2" high. *Smith collection. Photo by Don Blegen.* $150

Fig. 260. Milk glass; white shading to green; rust colored flowers with green leaves; base on three little flat feet. Similar to *Fig.* 312 in book I. Nutmeg burner; 8" high. *Cox collection. Photo by Karen & Keith Cox.* $375

Fig. 261. Light green satin glass lamp; enameled flowers in yellow and pink with green leaves and brown stems. Similar to *Fig.* 387 in book I. Acorn burner; 6" high. *Ness collection.* $625

Fig. 262. White milk glass; painted pink flowers and green leaves. Acorn burner; 7-1/4" high. Similar to *Fig.* 270 in book I. *Cox collection. Photo by Karen & Keith Cox.* $325

Fig. 263. Milk glass with ground carmel to light blue; fired on painted flowers in pink with green leaves. Nutmeg burner; 8" high. *Stewart collection. Photo by Tom Stewart.* $325

Fig. 264. Milk glass lamp with background painted light green; decorated with pink roses and green leaves. Paint not fired on and partly off. Nutmeg burner; 8" high. *Author's collection.* $300

Fig. 265. Milk glass; fired on paint around top of base and shade; floral pansy spray of purple and yellow flowers; green and gold leaves. Nutmeg burner; 8-1/2" high. *Solverson collection. Photo by Van Skiver's Studio.* $200

Fig. 266. Eight-paneled base and shade lamp. Milk glass; ground mottled in beige and cream; embossed rib around top and bottom of shade base; embossed rib separating each panel. painted leaves in brown and dark green; small blue berries. three small raised feet on bottom of base. Signed Feb 27, 1877. Similar to *Fig.* 129-130 in book I. Nutmeg burner; 7-1/2" high. *Bartol collection. Photo by Cox Studio.* $250

Fig. 267. White milk glass lamp paneled with multi-colored flowers. gold paint around top and bottom of embossing. Dresden mark on bottom. Also comes painted with wind-mill scene in blue. Made by Pairpoint Glass Co., New Bedford, Mass. ca. 1896. Acorn burner; 8-1/4" high. *Author's collection.* $700

Fig. 268. White milk glass lamp; applied handle; matching ball shade. Wreath decoration on wick-raiser. Foreign burner; 6" high. *Caskey collection. By Ramsdell's Photo.* $250

Fig. 269. White milk glass with matching chimney. Applied handle. Olmsted type burner; 4" high. *Feltner collection. Photo by David B. Grim.* $275

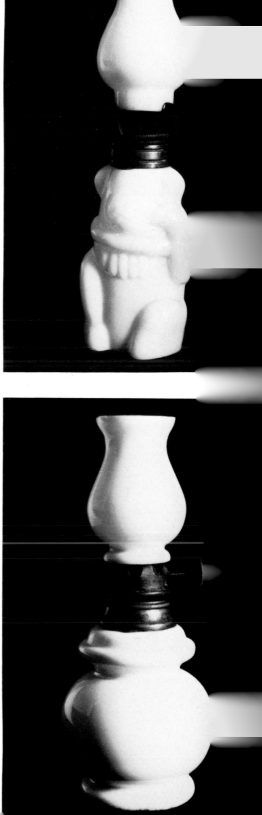

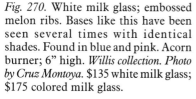

Fig. 270. White milk glass; embossed melon ribs. Bases like this have been seen several times with identical shades. Found in blue and pink. Acorn burner; 6" high. *Willis collection. Photo by Cruz Montoya.* $135 white milk glass; $175 colored milk glass.

Fig. 271. White milk glass lamp; figure of a bear. Foreign burner; 5-1/2" high. *Schafer collection. Photo by James Hulsebus.* $265

Fig. 272. White milk glass; matching chimney-shade. Wrong burner, or chimney-shade on burner wrong. Foreign burner; 5-1/2" high. *Hulsebus collection. Photo by James Hulsebus.* $135

Fig. 273. Milk glass lamp; white with figures of children in colors of pink, blue, and white. Foreign burner; 8" high. *Schafer collection. Photo by James Hulsebus.* $550

Fig. 274. Milk glass shoe; no handle. See *Fig.* 51 in book I. Made by Atterbury & Co. of Pittsburgh, Pa. ca. 1860. Hornet burner; 3-1/2" high. *Rodney collection.* $770

Fig. 275. Brass pedestal base; milk glass shade. Nutmeg burner; 7" to top of shade. *Rapai collection. Photo by Frank Lambert.* $135

Fig. 276. Brass pedestal base; reproduction, milk glass shade. Nutmeg burner; 5" high. *Creekman collection. Photo by Archie Johnson.* $75

Fig. 277. Brass saucer hand lamp; heavily embossed design; applied handle; green cased glass shade; spots on shade are reflections from camera. Referred to as the "No. 888 Hand Lamp" in the P & A catalog. ca. 1906. Center-draft Royal burner; 8-3/8" high. *McWright collection. Photo by Frank L. McWright.* $175

Fig. 278. Brass pedestal lamp; heavily embossed ribs vertical and horizontal; brass shade rest on chimney. Acorn burner; 7" high. *Miller collection. Aurora Photo.* $95

Fig. 279. Pewter pedestal base lamp with removable clear glass oil font. See bottom; heavily embossed with various decorations, and "Antique" musical instruments; ribbed white milk glass shade; (shade may or may not be original) Base, and wick-raiser marked "R. Ditmar, Wien." Foreign burner; 11" high. *Stewart collection. Photo by Tom Stewart.* $275

Fig. 280. Jr. Rochester Lamp; embossed brass; embossed ribbed milk glass shade; (shade may or may not be original) signed Pat'd Setp. 14, 1886. Unmarked burner; 12" high. *Stewart collection. Photo by Tom Stewart.* $210

Fig. 281. Nickel-plated pedestal base lamp; heavily embossed design on base and font; straight ribbed cased glass shade in rose shading to light. Signed Bradley and Hubbard Lamp; marked on font "the B & H Pat. May 3, 1892." B. & H. burner; 12-1/2" high. *Solverson collection. Photo by Van Skiver's Studio.* $420

Fig. 282. Pedestal base lamp; brass with embossed design of leaves around base and shade. Blue, red and amber glass jewels in shade. Foreign burner; 11" high. *Hulsebus collection. Photo by James Hulsebus.* $165

Fig. 283. Brass pedestal saucer base; hammered effect design in bottom of saucer; embossed design around font; shade in green cased glass. Spots on shade are reflections from camera. Nutmeg burner; 8-1/2" high. *von Linden collection. Toles Photo.* $110

Fig. 284. Brass, pedestal base lamp, cased glass shade in aqua. Foreign burner; 10-1/2" high. *Hulsebus collection. Photo by James Hulsebus.* $150

Fig. 285. Brass pedestal lamp with embossed design bands; shade has glass jewels, green, topaz and amethyst. Green beaded fringe around shade. Wrong shade holder. Brevete burner; 10" high. *Rosenberger collection. Photo by David B. Grim.* $155

Fig. 286. Pedestal base brass lamp; heavily embossed design; red and green jewels in shade trimmed with a white beaded fringe. Probably wrong shade-holder. Kosmos Brenner burner; 11-1/2" high. *Willis collection. Photo by Cruz Montoya.* $155

Fig. 287. Pedestal base brass lamp with embossed design on font. Shade has red and blue glass jewels. Foreign unmarked burner; 8-1/2" high. *Battersby collection.* $145

Fig. 288. Brass pedestal base lamp; embossed wreaths and swags. Shade has large glass jewels of yellow, red, and blue set in the middle of alternating wreaths. Foreign burner; 11" high. *Feltner collection. Photo by David B. Grim.* $315

Fig. 289. Brass pedestal base lamp; applied handle; embossed leaves around bottom of shade; glass jewels in amethyst, blue and green. Trimmed with fringe of amber beads. Signed "Pigeon." Foreign burner; 10" high. *Oswald collection. Photo by Cliff's Studio.* $85

Fig. 290. Pedestal base lamp; Left, assembled; base and top of font embossed design in gold colored thin, sharp, tin. Bristol glass font with paintings in natural colors of an owl on a tree limb surrounded by leaves. Moon in background. Right, unassembled; showing the unusual removable oil font. Shade missing. Nutmeg burner; 9" high. *Bailey collection. Photo by Dick Bailey.* $250

Fig. 291. Nickel-plated brass lamp signed "Lampe-Pigeon." Camphor-finished shade with a veined surfaced flora band pattern in blue, yellow and green. Evidently, the lamp is old and came with the standard clear glass shade instead of the present one. Aug. 1979. Identical lamp was sold at auction with same type shade; apparently shade is all right. Foreign burner; 9-1/2" high. *McWright collection. Photo by Frank L. McWright.* $135

Fig. 292. Brass saucer stem lamp; signed Pat. Feb. 27,1877. Shade missing. Nutmeg burner; 9" high. *Willis collection. Photo by Cruz Montoya.* $125

Fig. 293. Lamp-post style fluid lamp in nickel-plated brass; heavily embossed ribs around bottom; white milk glass hanging font; font unscrews from hanger for filling. 7-1/8" high. *McWright collection. Photo by Frank L. McWright.* $190

Fig. 294. Brass stem and base lamp; white milk glass shade. Marked A.R.Co. "Pat. 7, '23." Made in U.S.A. burner; 10" high. *Oswald collection. Photo by Cliff's Studio.* $125

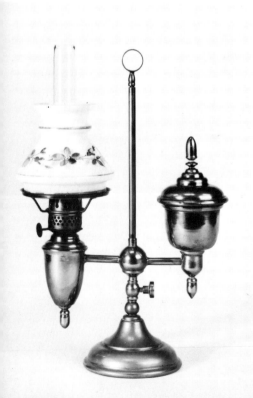

Fig. 295. Advertisement (Ca. 1890) for "The New Student Night Lamp." Manufactured by the Bristol Brass and Clock Co.; Bristol, Conn. Geo. W. Brown was the firm's agent in New York City.

Fig. 296. Salesman sample for demonstration. Brass & Single Student Lamp." Signed on font "Pillischer." Tank mechanism separate. White bristol shade. Kleiman burner; 12" high. *Shryock collection. Photo by Poist't Studio.* $900

Fig. 297. Brass "Single Acorn Student Lamp." White bristol shade; fired on painted flowers in pink and red with green leaves. Nutmeg burner; 10" high. *Shryock collection. Photo by Poist's Studio.* $950

Fig. 298. Brass single student lamp. Yellow milk glass shade. Cap signed "B & H." Nutmeg burner; 12-1/2" high to top of finger-ring. *Shryock collection. Photo by Poist's Studio.* $800

Fig. 299. Student Lamp. Brass, adjustable heights. White milk glass shade. Foreign burner; 12-1/4" to top of finger-ring. *Cox collection. Photo by Gary Studio.* $900

Fig. 300. Brass student lamp; white bristol shade. Foreign burner; 12" high. *Author's collection. Photo by Poist's Studio.* $400

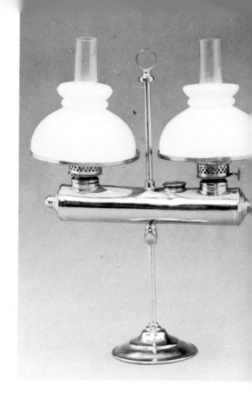

Fig. 301. Double brass student lamp. Adjustable heights. White bristol shades. Foreign burners; 12" to top of supporting stand. *Cox collection. Photo by Gary Studio.* $525

Fig. 302. Brass log double student lamp. White milk glass shades. Similar to *Fig.* 87 in book I. No markings. Nutmeg burners; 11-1/2" high. *Cotting collection. Photo by Sisson Studio.* $925

Fig. 303. Brass "Double Barrel Student Stand Lamp." Signed B. and H. on cap. Pink milk glass shades. Nutmeg burner; 10" high. *Shryock collection. Photo by Poist's Studio.* $1475

Fig. 304. Brass "Double Acorn Student Stand Lamp." Marked on bottom "Pat Jan. 31, 1871, Aug. 31, 1873." Yellow milk glass shades. Nutmeg burners; 10-1/2" high. *Shryock collection. Photo by Poist's Studio.* $2100

Fig. 305. Brass double sleigh lamp: the filler cap is the extension rod. Standard, signed Lincoln Pat, "Oct. 28, '79." Nutmeg burner; 9-7/8" to top of ring. 7-1/2" long from front runner to back of tank. *Shryock collection. Photo by Poist's Studio.* $950

Fig. 306. Brass sleigh lamp. Signed "Oct. 29, '79." White milk glass shade painted fired-on pink. Nutmeg burner; 5" high. *Author's collection. Photo by Poist's Studio.* $800

Fig. 307. Brass barrel bracket lamp; signed Lincoln Pat, "Oct. 28, '79." White milk glass shade. Nutmeg burner; 6" from bottom of tank to top of chimney; tank is 3-3/8" wide. *Shryock collection. Photo by Poist's Studio.* $770

Opposite page, top left: Fig. 308. Brass single-burner log pig-type lamp. Attached pan for holding spices over the chimney for scenting the room. Signed on side, Oct. 29, '79." See *Fig.* 81 in book I. Nutmeg burner; 8" high. *Author's collection. Photo by Poist's Studio.* $525

Top right: Fig. 309. Time lamp. Clear glass; embossed "Grand Val's Perfect Time Indicator" and time marks 8 to 6; reverse side (shown) embossed Eagle; white milk glass bee-hive shade. It is quite possible the "tall variation" are the earlier of the Time Indicating Lamps, however there is no proof. Similar to *Fig. 23* in book I. Unmarked burner; 8" high. *McWright collection. Photo by Frank L. McWright.* $350

Bottom right: Fig. 310. The Weaver Time Lamp. This lamp is more slender than *Fig. 23* in book I. Around the base is marked " The Weaver Time Lamp." The burner is the same as on other time lamps. Milk glass bee-hive shade. It is higher than other time lamps. Unmarked burner. 8" high. *Author's collection.* $375

NIGHT CLOCK No. 7—Wit

Fig. 311. Kerosene Illuminated Night Clock. These clocks used a small lamp or a coil of thin candle. Some were lighted by a small gas jet. They were dated in the 1890s and were made in France. The face was a translucent porcelain ring. Timepieces quartly of the American Clock and Watch Foundation. Vol. 1, No. 4. Feb. 1950. $1500

Fig. 312. German clock with alarm lamp. Pewter and brass base. Applied feet and handle; frosted shade with a fleur-de-lis design with cupid pointing to Roman numerals in black. Unmarked burner; 6-1/2" high. *Schafer collection. Photo by David J. Lans.* $1225

Fig. 313. Brass tray lamp; plain font; embossed ribs around the top and embossed design on tray with applied feet; hammered effect design in bottom of tray. Shade heavily embossed with hammered-type pattern shading from amber to fuschia and blue. **Note:** May or may not be original, but combination looks nice. Nutmeg burner; 6-1/4" high. *Bartol collection. Photo by Cox Studio.* $125

Fig. 314. Brass tray lamp; plain font; embossed ribs around top; embossed design on tray with applied feet; hammered-effect design in bottom of tray that matches shade hanging on chimney. **Note:** This type shade original for several have been seen. Nutmeg burner; 6-1/2" high. *Author's collection.* $175

Fig. 315. Tree stump lamp in shape of an anvil embossed; with attached horse-shoe and hammer. Inside porcelain, outside fired on paint, black trimmed in dull gold; gold largely washed off. Milk glass shade. Nutmeg burner; 8" high. *Author's collection.* $200

Fig. 316. Beer barrel lamp. Cast iron painted black; double filler holds cork-capped. Ends of barrel signed "E. W. Voight Detroit Trade Mark Pilsen Beer." Hornet burner; 4" high. *McWright collection. Photo by Frank L. McWright.* $500

Fig. 317. Bisque base. Monkey in dark and light gray. Barrel and bands brown with nail heads in gold. Shade and chimney missing. Foreign burner; 3-1/4" high. *Boles collection.* $250

Fig. 318. Porcelain base; Monkey climbing a clump of salmon-colored bamboo stalks; gold bands and dull green foliage. Unmarked burner; 4-1/2" high. Don't know if this base had a shade at one time. *Feltner collection. Photo by David B. Grim.* $275

Fig. 319. Reclining camel base; in tan luster finish porcelain. On bottom marked, Germany number 7049; probably had foreign collar and burner originally; 5-1/8" high. Nutmeg burner. Shade and chimney missing. *Feltner collection. Photo by David B. Grim.* $450

Fig. 320. Brown and green porcelain base, white spitz, muzzled dog with amber glass eyes; Supposed to be part of a Staffordsire figural series; shade missing. English burner; 8" to top of burner. Similar to *Fig.* 496 in book I. *Feltner collection. Photo by David B. Grim.* $650

Fig. 321. "Lady Fox" base, sporting a coral colored hat, bedecked with blue forget-me-nots and pink roses. She is wearing a lavender, fur-trimmed coat over a coral colored ruffled skirt and holds a dark green pocketbook. English registry mark 87026. Probably made by R. Plant or S.L. Plant of Longton, Staffordshire in 1887. English burner; 6-5/8" to top of collar. Shade and chimney missing. *Feltner collection. Photo by David B. Grim.* $725

Fig. 322. Base brown glazed pug dog sitting on a tasseled pillow; on bottom of base are marks of crossed swords with a number 4236. Shade and chimney are missing. Spar-Brenner burner; 6" to top of burner. *Feltner collection. Photo by David B. Grim.* $650

Fig. 323. Porcelain dog embossed; applied handle, green. With deeply embossed green diamond quilted shade. Foreign burner; 7" to top of shade. *Reith collection. Photo by Michael Clifton.* $575

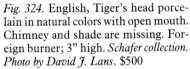

Fig. 324. English, Tiger's head porcelain in natural colors with open mouth. Chimney and shade are missing. Foreign burner; 3" high. *Schafer collection. Photo by David J. Lans.* $500

Fig. 325. Porcelain, Ram's head in natural colors; clear glass shade with three feathers marked "Perfect Candle Lamp." Foreign burner; 7-1/2" high. Schafer collection. *Photo by David J. Lans.* $675

Fig. 326. Majolica chicken tree stump lamp bases. Stumps greenish brown. Hen on one stump; rooster on other stump; fired on paint. Chickens brown and gray with pink beaks and feet; red comb and wattles. Chimneys clear glass. Shades missing. Foreign burner with diamonds and dots; 5" high. *Author's collection.* $675

Fig. 327. White bisque swan lamp; base light blue with swan holding a light-pink egg; painted and enameled in blue, red, and green; orange flowers; light green bristol shade. Foreign burner; 8-1/2" high. *Stewart collection.* *Photo by Tom Stewart.* $700

Fig. 328. Elephant porcelain base, in natural tannish-gray color seated on a base varying from green to tan and brown. Has registry number. Supposed to be part of figural series. Shade and chimney missing. Foreign burner. 9-1/4" high. *Feltner collection. Photo by David B. Grim.* $525

Fig. 329. Porcelain base. Elephant painted gray, green, blue, and orchid. Markings on base R.D. 102612. Shade and chimney missing. Unmarked burner. 5-1/2" high. *Boles collection.* $600

Fig. 330. Elephant with dog attached; porcelain all in natural colors, and ivy decorations; shade satin glass with ivy decorations. Foreign burner; 9-1/2" high. *Schafer collection. Photo by David J. Lans.* $600

Fig. 331. Bisque lamp; base with full figure, winged cherub in flesh tones with a pale lavender ground, yellow door, and white butterfly; cranberry glass shade, embossed diamond quilted pattern. Base signed "3387." Foreign burner; 6" high. *McWright collection. Photo by Frank L. McWright.* $415

Fig. 332. Porcelain base; applied 3-full figure cherubs, trimmed in gold. Multicolor floral sprays with a pale blue wash at top. Shade of white milk glass trimmed in gold with same multicolor floral sprays and a pale green wash at top and bottom. Kosmos burner; 12-1/4" high. *McWright collection. Photo by Frank L. McWright.* $525

Fig. 333. Dresden base in mottled brown strewn with applied flowers. Basket-weave font supported by cupids with applied flowers and leaves. Milk glass shade splashed with pink and blue flowers; green leaves. Challenge burner; 12-1/4" high. *Feltner collection. Photo by David B. Grim.* $825

Fig. 334. White china base; flowers green and pale peach applied. Embossed design with cupid heads. Hornet burner; 4" high. Shade and chimney missing. *Boles collection.* $150

Fig. 335. Dresden china lamp; embossed design pink trimmed in gold. Applied pink flowers and green leaves with applied handles. Applied cherub on base; matching shade with crystal prisms. Foreign burner; 8" high. *Cox collection. Photo by Karen & Keith Cox.* $550

Fig. 336. Jasperware; green base with white Oriental figure; white bristol-type shade. Spots on shade are reflections from camera. Foreign burner; 6-1/2" high. *McWright collection. Photo by Frank L. McWright.* $600

Fig. 337. Porcelain, English Moore. Girl and boy dressed very colorful. Etched floral shades. Foreign burner; 8" high. *Schafer collection. Photo by David J. Lans.* $800

Fig. 338. China lamp. China boy pushing an embossed corn pattern font on an embossed design wheelbarrow; in colors of yellow, blue and pink with gold trim; milk glass ball shade. Nutmeg burner; 7-1/2" high. *Burke collection. Photo by Archie Johnson.* $475

Fig. 339. China boy pushing embossed corn pattern font lamp, on embossed design wheelbarrow in multi-colors; brown wicker shade lined with light peach silk. Acorn burner; 7-1/2" high. *Author's collection.* $475

174

Fig. 340. China lamp; boy standing in front of cottage painted in multi-colors trimmed in gold. Brown wicker shade lined with a light peach cloth. Acorn burner; 8" high. *Author's collection.* $475

Fig. 341. China lamp base; heavily embossed design with delicate painted multi-colored angels on a green leaf. Brown wicker shade lined with ivory cloth. Acorn burner; 8" high. *Author's collection.* $550

Fig. 342. Bisque girl with cart; painted in ivory, blue, yellow, and other colors. Fired on enamel ivory metal cut-out design shade. See *Fig.* 485 in book I. Acorn burner; 9" high. *Solverson collection. Photo by Van Skiver's Studio.* $500

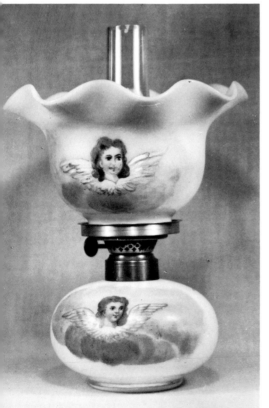

Fig. 343. Lamb base. Feet on dark platform; three applied angels painted blue and pink, peeping out of a white bisque body of a lamb. Marked on collar patented March 21, 1878. Hornet burner; 5-1/4" high. *Willis collection. Photo by Cruz Montoya.* $400

Fig. 344. Bisque child wrapped in blanket forming a peach colored base; trimmed in light blue and tan with an embossed design and dots. Shade and chimney missing. Roitner-Wien with a wing burner. 4-1/2" high. *Boles collection.* $400

Fig. 345. White bristol glass lamp with fired on paintings of angels in pastel colors of blue, brown, beige, and orange. Apparently, two different artists painted the shade and base. It is believed to be old and original. Hornet type burner with 6 stars. 6" high. *Author's collection.* $165

Fig. 346. Blue glass; Mary Gregory type with white enamel cherubs and flowers. Eight-pointed star on burner. Foreign burner; 6-1/2" high. *Bartol collection. Photo by Cox Studio.* $850

Fig. 347. Mary Gregory type lamp; enameled figure of boy in white; light green glass with inside ribbing; darker green chimney may not be original. Acorn burner; 4" high. *Stewart collection. Photo by Tom Stewart.* $165

Fig. 348. Mary Gregory-type; blue glass with clear chimney; white enamel boy and flowers. May or may not have had a shade. Acorn burner; 10" high. *Cox collection. Photo by Karen & Keith Cox.* $165

Fig. 349. Santa Claus lamp. Milk glass; fired-on paint has been sprayed on uniformly but rather carelessly applied. Brick-red color around base of shade over Santa's cap and on his pack. Face and eyes largely white. Gunmetal color on the boots shading lighter on the toes and ground. There is an indentation in the bottom of the base unlike the usual Santa Clause which is perfectly flat. See picture above for bottom of base with the indentation, and the flat one. Shade is very thin glass. Probably made by same manufacturer, Consolidated Lamp and Glass Co., Pittsburgh, Pa. ca. 1894. See *Fig.* 8 in book I. Marked on burner, "P & A MFG Co." Nutmeg burner; 9-1/2" high. *Battersby collection.* $3500

Fig. 350. Portrait Lady Lamp. Milk glass; pale blue ground with gold trim circling portraits; portraits in flesh tones, brown hair, black and white. P & A Victor burner; 9" high. *McWright collection. Photo by Frank L. McWright.* $470

Fig. 351. Portrait Lady Lamp. White milk glass painted yellow; embossed design. Lady painted in various colors. Many variations of this style. See *Fig.* 291-295 in book I. P & A Victor burner; 8" high. *Schafer collection. Photo by David J. Lans.* $470

Fig. 352. Porcelain base with white milk glass shade; decorated with red roses, green leaves, and gilt trim; base and shade show four different scenes of Frankfort, Germany. Similar to *Fig.* 335 in book I. Kosmos burner; 11" high. *White collection. Photo by Frank L. McWright.* $510

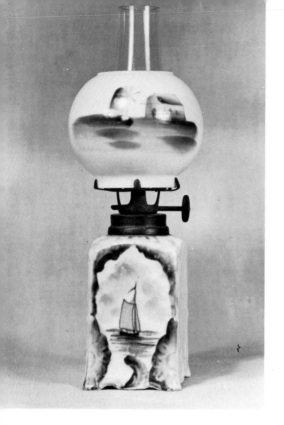

Fig. 353. Delph lamp. White porcelain base; white bristol shade. Boat and windmill scenes in blue. Foreign burner; 6" high. *Rodney collection.* $330

Fig. 354. Milk glass; white with black, gold and white seagulls; blue water, and green scope. Foreign burner; 6" high. *McWright collection. Photo by Frank L. McWright.* $370

Fig. 355. Delft lamp; porcelain base similar to *Fig.* 338 in book I. Splattered blueground, fading to white center panels. Two sides have embossed flower basket design, the other two sides have embossed cupids. Bristol shade originally had wind-mill house design in the Delft manner, now mostly worn off. Foreign burner; 6-1/4" high. *Feltner collection. Photo by David B. Grim.* $300

180

Fig. 356. Oriental decorated type lamp. Milk glass; ground red and orange with gold scrolls and flowers. Black and grey grasshoppers and leaves on one side of base and shade; on other side a bird and lotus blooms. Removable glass font. Foreign burner; 10-1/4" high. *Bartol collection. Photo by Cox Studio.* $500

Fig. 357. Milk glass lamp; white with dark green ground; lined with gold stripes at top and bottom; pale green leaves with light pink and maroon flowers. Foreign burner; 8-1/2" high. *McWright collection. Photo by Frank L. McWright.* $350

Fig. 358. Milk glass painted robin's egg blue; embossed flowers painted pink; green leaves and border around bottom of shade and font. Foreign burner; 8" high. *Stewart collection. Photo by Tom Stewart.* $420

Fig. 359. Milk glass with fired-on blue trim, pink and blue flowers; brown and green leaves. Foreign burner using round wick. Shade holder fits directly over wick spout and swivels. Wick turner has set of balanced scales embossed on it with two stars below. 8-1/4" to highest point of shade. *Feltner collection. Photo by David B. Grim.* $445

Fig. 360. White milk glass lamp; ground color and decorations in green, yellow, and rose shading to pink. Marked on bottom of base, made in France; 8 pointed star on wick-raiser. Foreign burner; 11" high. *Caskey collection. By Ramsdell's Photo.* $445

Fig. 361. Bristol white glass, covered with fired on light orchid paint around base and shade. Fired on painted flowers and decorations in various colors. Foreign burner; 9" high. *Boles collection.* $430

Fig. 362. Light green opaline glass lamp with fired on flowers in various colors; trimmed in gold. Foreign burner; 10" high. *Sandeen collection.* $500

Fig. 363. White opaline glass; decorated with dark blue flowers, gray-green foliage. Foreign burner; 10" high. *Rosenberger collection. Photo by David B. Grim.* $445

Fig. 364. Bristol glass, white fired on painted decorations in light and dark blue. Foreign burner; 9-1/2" high. *Boles collection.* $420

Fig. 365. Milk glass lamp; yellow on bottom and rose on top of base. Light yellow shading to pink on shade; painted blue flowers and green leaves. Spar-Brenner burner; 8-1/2" high. *Caskey collection. Photo by Ramsdell's Photo.* $370

Fig. 366. Milk glass; fired on paint, pale blue around top of shade and base; multi-colored flowers and green leaves. Schmidt-Jaedicke, Berlin on burner. Foreign burner; 10-1/2" high. *Carman collection. Logan Photo.* $365

Fig. 367. White bristol glass lamp; decorated with blue asters, red and coral flowers, with gold foliage. Foreign burner; 8-5/8" high. *Rosenberger collection. Photo by David B. Grim.* $430

Fig. 368. Milk glass lamp; with bands in blue, pink flowers and green leaves. Other decorations in gold and orange. Dietz Night Light burner; 8-1/4" high. *Rosenberger collection. Photo by David B. Grim.* $500

Fig. 369. Pedestal base lamp; light blue glass; top of font and bottom of shade trimmed in clear overshot; enameled green cactus leaves and red flowers. Foreign burner; 7" high. *Caskey collection. Photo by Ramsdell.* $600

Fig. 370. Bristol glass; lavender. Supposed to be English. Reflections in shade and base are from camera. Foreign burner; 8-1/4" high. *Schafer collection. Photo by David J. Lans.* $560

Fig. 371. Pedestal base with rows of heavy embossing; cobalt blue glass. Reflections on shade are from camera. Foreign burner: 9-1/4" high. *McWright collection. Photo by Frank L. McWright.* $375

Fig. 372. Blue milk glass; flowers and leaves in various colors. Spar-Brenner burner; 8" high. *Oswald collection. Photo by Cliff's Studio.* $285

Fig. 373. White milk glass; delicate floral decorations in purple, lavender and blue; embossed design on base. (shade not original). Foreign burner; 10" high. *Caskey collection. Photo by Ramsdell.* $80

Fig. 374. Bracket lamp; cast iron painted gold. Cranberry glass shade in optic honeycomb pattern. Foreign burner; 8-3/4" high. *McWright collection. Photo by Frank L. McWright.* $850

Fig. 375. Bracket lamp. Steel painted black; Cranberry glass base and chimney in a swirled optic pattern. Foreign burner; 7-3/4" high. *McWright collection. Photo by Frank L. McWright.* $550

Fig. 376. Hanging lamp brass; similar to a country store lamp; pleated shade matches middle font; milk glass chimney. Foreign burner; 7-1/2" to finger-ring at top of smoke bell. *Lemon collection. Photo by Wilmyer Studio.* $680

Fig. 377. Hanging lamp. Brass grocery store type with white milk glass shade. Acorn burner; 10" from bottom to top of hanging ring. *Cox collection. Photo by Gary Studio.* $775

Fig. 378. Miniature hall hanging lamp; brass chain and fixtures. Pink satin glass shade. Bottom pulls down to light. A small clear glass kerosene lamp with chimney enclosed. 20 " from bottom to top of chain. *Author's collection.* $725

Fig. 379. Hanging lamp, satin glass, deep rose shading to pink; nickel plated brass around top and bottom of shade. From top to bottom of lamp, 6-1/4". *Late Myers collection.* $780

Opposite page, top left: Fig. 380. Hanging lamp. White metal washed in brass. White bristol shade. 1-3/4" across bottom of shade. Clear beaded fringe. 3 candle-holders on side. Olmsted type unmarked burner; 8" to top of chain. *Battersby collection.* $1250

Top right: Fig. 381. Hanging lamp. Brass frame and chain; applied brass birds supposedly sitting on a tree limb on each side of font. Marked on bottom of base L. P. Lamp Co., Sample, '83. Embossed green glass shade in a cosmos-type pattern; green glass prisms. Lamp also similar to *Fig. 382*. May or may not be old. Acorn burner; 11-1/4" from bottom to top of hanging ring. *Carman collection. Photo by Logan.* $1250 (if old).

Bottom right: Fig. 382. Hanging lamp. Brass frame and chain; applied brass birds sitting on supposedly a tree limb on each side of font. Marked on bottom of font, Sample Sept. 2, '78. Embossed milk glass shade similar to shade in *Fig. 396* in book I. Clear glass prisms. Lamp also similar to *Fig. 381*. May or may not be old. Marked P & A Mfg. Co. Corp burner; 10" to top of hanging finger-ring. *Cox collection. Photo by Gary Studio.* $1350 (if old).

Fig. 383. Hanging lamp. All brass frame; signed "Pat'd Dec 9, 90—Sep, 29, 96" on the decoration bottom of frame. Cranberry glass shade in the optic honeycomb pattern; clear glass font with clear glass prisms. Acorn burner; 12" to top. *McWright collection. Photo by Frank L. McWright.* $2000

Fig. 384. Hanging lamp. Brass frame and chain; bottom of font marked "Sample". Pairpoint type shade embossed with puffed-out fruits in various colors. May or may not be old. Acorn burner; 11" from bottom to top of hanging ring. *Cox collection. Photo by Gary Studio.* $900 (if old).

Fig. 385. Boudoir lamp. Brass base; fluted stem; brass cut-out design pattern shade lined with pink silk and Mica. (Isinglass). Trimmed with a beaded fringe. Acorn burner; 10-1/2" high. *McWright collection. Photo by Frank L. McWright.* $100

Fig. 386. Boudoir lamp. Brass round stem and base; brass shade cut-out pattern design; lined with yellow silk and Mica. (Isinglass). Trimmed with a beaded fringe. Acorn burner; 10-1/4" high. *McWright collection. Photo by Frank L. McWright.* $100

Fig. 387. White metal pedestal base lamp with embossed design. Sterling silver cut-out design shade lined with pale pink linen and mica. Clear glass beaded fringe. Acorn burner; 10-3/4" high. *Author's collection.* $110

Fig. 388. Brass wall hanging lamp. Sterling silver with a cut-out design shade of red linen and mica lining; red glass beaded fringe. Acorn burner; 13" from bottom to top of font. *Author's collection.* $175

Fig. 389. Candle-stick peg lamp. Embossed design brass base with applied handle. Cut-out design silver shade lined with linen and mica. Trimmings of glass beads around shade. Candle-stick milk glass. Acorn burner; on top of shade holder "Twi-light". 11" high; base 3-1/4". *Sandeen collection.* $690

Fig. 390. Peg lamps. Embossed blue glass bases (candle holders) decorated with multi-color flowers and trimmed in gold. Applied feet and finger-holes. Bristol glass fonts with pegs at bottom. Brown wicker shades lined in a beige silk-like material. Acorn burner; 7-1/2" high. *Author's collection. Photo by Poist's Studio.* $225

Fig. 391. Glow peg lamp. Milk glass peg font has glass wick holder like the one on *Fig.* 627 in book I. Attached shade holder has "Glolite" on top. Silver cut-out design pattern with peach colored mica and linen; trimmed with a fringe of clear glass beads. Mercury base with embossed pattern; removable peg fonts. See *Fig.* 627 in book I for string-type burner. 11-3/4" high. *Author's collection.* $250

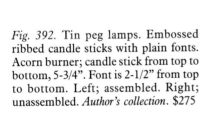

Fig. 392. Tin peg lamps. Embossed ribbed candle sticks with plain fonts. Acorn burner; candle stick from top to bottom, 5-3/4". Font is 2-1/2" from top to bottom. Left; assembled. Right; unassembled. *Author's collection.* $275

Fig. 393. Peg lamp. Brass saucer "candle-holder" base; applied handle; removable peg-stick font milk glass. May or may not have had a shade. Nutmeg burner: 6-1/2" high. *Creekman collection. Photo by Archie Johnson.* $80

Fig. 394. Candle-stick lamp. China saucer base decorated in blue and brown. Font decorated brass; white porcelain candle stick; embossed ribbed swirl pattern. Foreign burner with 7 pointed star; 8-3/4" high. *Rodney collection.* $475

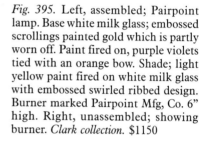

Fig. 395. Left, assembled; Pairpoint lamp. Base white milk glass; embossed scrollings painted gold which is partly worn off. Paint fired on, purple violets tied with an orange bow. Shade; light yellow paint fired on white milk glass with embossed swirled ribbed design. Burner marked Pairpoint Mfg, Co. 6" high. Right, unassembled; showing burner. *Clark collection.* $1150

Fig. 396. Milk glass lavender base; embossed ribbing and design around bottom; white bristol-type shade with embossed ribbing. DRGM collar and burner; 7-1/2" high. *McWright collection. Photo by Frank L. McWright.* $420

Fig. 397. Milk glass; fired on paint; dark green at top of base and shade; pink roses trimmed with a beaded fringe. Nutmeg burner; 7-1/4" high. *McDonald collection. Photo by Ann Gilbert McDonald.* $445

Fig. 398. Satin glass; white with embossed shell design; painted red with blue flowers. Hornet burner; 7-3/4" high. *Cox collection. Photo by Karen & Keith Cox.* $3350

Fig. 399. White satin glass; embossed swirled ribs at bottom separated by brown lines; embossed petal design; decorated with painted forget-me-nots. 4" high. *Duris collection. Photo by Lincoln McCabe.* $80

Fig. 400. Cobalt blue glass; enameled decorations on shade; shade and base identical in color. May or may not be original. Nutmeg burner; marked P. & A. 6-1/2" high. *Carman collection. Logan Photo.* $175

Fig. 401. Cobalt blue; embossed pattern. Found in cranberry glass. Foreign burner; 7-1/2" high. *Terrio collection. Photo by Poist's Studio.* $500

Fig. 402. White bristol glass; accent bands edged in black; floral bands in blue, yellow and orange. Foreign burner; 5" high. *McWright collection. Photo by Frank L. McWright.* $445

Fig. 403. Pink cased satin glass with melon-ribbed base and petal ball shade. See *Fig.* 385, 389, and 390 in book I. This combination has been seen in different states and in different colors so it could be original. Made by Consolidated Lamp and Glass Co., Pittsburgh, Pa. about 1894. Nutmeg burner; 7" high. *Author's collection.* $650

Fig. 404. Red satin glass with embossed shell motif on base and shade. P. & A. Victor burner: 12" high. *White collection. Photo by Frank L. McWright.* $675

Fig. 405. Porcelain base, with bristol shade decorated with orange, blue and lavender flowers; embossed scrolling with spattered gold trim. Marked Victoria-Carlsbad-Austria. Nutmeg burner; 8-1/2" high. *Feltner collection. Photo by David B. Grim.* $510

Fig. 406. Milk glass; white with orange roses and green leaves; gold band around base. Foreign burner; 7-1/4" high. *McWright collection. Photo by Frank L. McWright.* $220

Fig. 407. Milk glass; fired on floral decorations of red roses and wild flowers with green leaves; green leaf wreath encircles shade. Foreign burner; 8-3/4" high. *Solverson collection. Photo by Van Skiver's Studio.* $340

Fig. 408. Porcelain font on brass footed base; embossed birds and flowers. Hand painted Chinese motif. Signed. Shade missing. Nutmeg burner; 5-1/4" high. *Stewart collection. Photo by Tom Stewart.* $120

Fig. 409. Cranberry shading to light, threaded glass base; decorated with enameled white flowers and leaves. Shade matching in color. May or may not be original. Foreign burner; 8-1/4" high. *Cox collection. Photo by Gary Studio.* $110

Fig. 410. Art Nouveau copper lamp with fittings for shade of similar style and proportions as *Fig. 251* in book I. 3" to top of shade holder. *Feltner collection. Photo by David B. Grim.* $475

Fig. 411. Amber glass, faintly paneled on pewter pedestal base. Chimney has original trademark remaining, "Cristalline". "Made in France". Foreign burner; 8-1/4" high. *Rosenberger collection. Photo by David B. Grim.* $460

Fig. 412. Blue-green glass stem lamp; embossed design with original chimney. Rare. Nutmeg burner; 9" high. *Schafer collection. Photo by David J. Lans.* $425

Fig. 413. Hand lamp. Red glass "Bohemian" cut to clear design of berries and leaves. Applied clear glass handle. Found in cobalt blue. Hornet burner; 9-1/4" to top of shade. *Sensel collection.* $630

Fig. 414. Amber glass " Bohemian" cut to clear design. Enameled flowers, and decorations in white. Acorn burner: 7" high. *Boles collection.* $125

Fig. 415. Metal pedestal base; blue glass font with enameled flowers in pink with white leaves. Shade and chimney missing. Foreign burner; 7-3/4" high. *Bartol collection*. $95

Fig. 416. Brass pedestal lamp; frosted etched design shade; Spar-Brenner burner; 8" high. *Miller collection. Aurora Photo*. $195

Fig. 417. Square base gadroon design silver plated lamp beautifully engraved design of leaves and scrolls. Frosted ball shade with etched fleur-de-lis. Lamp signed Nappin & Webb's Princes Plate, London-Sheffield and bears hallmark. Silver plated Kosmos Brenner burner: 10-1/4" high. *Feltner collection. Photo by David B. Grim*. $650

Fig. 418. Delft base square with two handles; painted in the same colors and scenes, and signed with the Delft mark. Foreign burner; 4" high. *Duris collection. Photo by Lincoln McCabe.* $95

Fig. 419. Pedestal base lamp; porcelain embossed design trimmed in blue and white. Milk glass shade fired on paint scene of boat and windmill in shades of blue. May or may not be original. P. & A. Victor burner; 14-1/2" high. *Semprini collection. Photo by Frank L. McWright.* $575

Fig. 420. Three-tier banquet lamp; Delft; white milk glass; embossed and painted design of windmills and ship in matching colors of blues. P. & A. Victor burner; 15" high. *Stewart collection. Photo by Tom Stewart.* $700

Fig. 421. Three-tier banquet milk glass lamp; brass pedestal base, ribbed stem, lobulated font. Decorated with varigated flowers. P. & A. Victor burner; 15-3/4" high. *Rosenberger collection. Photo by David B. Grim.* $840

Fig. 422. Banquet lamp; brass filigree with removable oil font. Cranberry Dragon shade; marked "H. & B". P. & A. burner; 16-1/2" high. *Schafer collection. Photo by David J. Lans.* $700

Fig. 423. Three-tier banquet lamp; brass pedestal base; yellow satin glass, heavily embossed design pattern; milk glass shade, white with gold laurel wreath and fleur-de-lis decorations. Referred to as the "Elite Princess" in an 1899 advertisement by Consolidated Lamp. Found in pink, blue, and green satin glass; in pink, blue, and yellow milk glass shades, also ornate ruffled silk-shades. P. & A. burner; 17" high. *McWright collection. Photo by Frank L. McWright.* $575

Fig. 424. Milk glass white; with pink colorful floral decorations. Gold plated pedestal base; supposed to be Pairpoint. Nutmeg burner; 12" high. *Schafer collection. Photo by David J. Lans.* $950

Fig. 425. Pedestal base lamp; silver plated; embossed decorations of scrolls, florals and shells; frosted shade. W. & W. Kosmos burner: 12-1/2" high. *Burke collection. Photo by Archie Johnson.* $450

Fig. 426. Brass pedestal base; signed NB & IW, Reading, Pa. Metal font painted dark green and has a removable oil font. Shade embossed molded cased glass of yellow over crystal; etched to form yellow water-lilies on a frosted crystal ground. P. & A. Victor burner; 13-1/8" high. *Feltner collection. Photo by David B. Grim.* $735

Fig. 427. Elegant brass base lamp with font and lower pedestal of cobalt porcelain, decorated with applied brass garlands of flowers and ribbons. Top brass portion decorated with a band of embossed leaves; P & A Victor burner; 6-7/8" high. Burner, chimney and shade missing. *Feltner collection. Photo by David B. Grim.* $130

Fig. 428. Square base pedestal silver lamp, heavily embossed ribs; Burmese shade and chimney. Hinks & Son burner; 9-3/4" high. *Bartol collection. Photo by Cox Studio.* $1250

Fig. 429. Silver base; embossed triangle ribbed with applied fancy embossed feet; removable font. Peachblow satin glass shade. Foreign burner; 9-1/8" high. *Schafer collection. Photo by David J. Lans.* $1275

Fig. 430. Satin glass; mother-of-pearl, diamond pattern; pink shading to white. Brass pedestal base with curved handle. Found in apricot shading to white. Foreign burner; 10-3/4" high. *McWright collection. Photo by Frank L. McWright.* $2000

Fig. 431. Black wrought-iron base; removable brass font; cased glass shade yellow decorated with gold Fleur-de-Lis. Spots are reflections from camera. P. & A. Victor burner; 12" high. *Creekman collection. Photo by Archie Johnson.* $475

Fig. 432. Jr. Banquet lamp. Brass-plated pedestal base and font; white cased glass shade with gold dragon decorations. Base signed "Pairpoint". P. & A. Victor burner; 13-3/4" high. *White collection. Photo by Frank L. McWright.* $575

Fig. 433. Multi-color Cloisenne font on Marble base; frosted shade decorated in gold; spots on shade are reflections from camera. Foreign burner; 11-1/2" high. *Schafer collection. Photo by David J. Lans.* $1250

Fig. 434. Brass pedestal base; white porcelain font decorated with multi-colored flowers; trimmed in green with applied green rope handles. Removable copper font. Clambroth-type-glass shade in golden amber color with painted gold dragons and fleur-de-lis. spots on shade are reflections from camera. A. & P. Victor burner; 12" high. *Rodney collection.* $675

Fig. 435. Jr. Banquet lamp. Cast metal and tin washed in gold. Heavily embossed design on base and feet; removable brass font. Yellow cased glass shade. P. & A. Victor burner; 11-1/2" high. *McWright collection. Photo by Frank L. McWright.* $725

Fig. 436. Silver base with embossed flowers and ferns; shade frosted with etched design. Foreign burner; 9-1/2" high. *Schafer collection. Photo by David J. Lans.* $675

Fig. 437. Pewter pedestal lamp; embossed and heavily decorated base with removable glass font. Frosted glass decorated shade. Foreign burner; 9-1/2" high. *Schafer collection. Photo by James Hulsebus.* $300

Fig. 438. Brass plated pedestal base; metal font finished in textured moss green and tan to give a pottery look. Metal leaves and flowers in gold encase the font; removable brass oil font. yellow cased glass shade decorated with gold scrolling and flowers. P. & A. Victor burner; 13-1/2" high. *Feltner collection. Photo by David B. Grim.* $700

Fig. 439. Porcelain owl base lamp; natural colors. Cased glass yellow shade. Reflections of camera lights show eyes in shade. Foreign burner; 11" high. *Schafer collection. Photo by David J. Lans.* $925

Fig. 440. Porcelain owl base lamp; embossed with a satin glass yellow embossed ribbed shade; base marked "Made in Germany," burner marked Veritas Lamp Works, London. Foreign burner; 13-1/2" high. *Caskey collection. By Ramsdell's Photo.* $725

Fig. 441. White china owl base standing on brownish colored china rock. Glass eyes glued on. Burner and shade missing. Takes a foreign burner; 7-1/8" high. *Cotting collection. Photo by Sisson Studio.* $675

Fig. 442. Owl head lamp; porcelain; fired on paint in light blue and tan. Shade and chimney missing. English burner; 4" high. *Boles collection.* $350

Fig. 443. Owl lamp base; frosted green at top; shading to clear at bottom. Shade and chimney missing. Foreign burner; 6-1/2" high. *Rosenberger collection. Photo by David B. Grim.* $600

Fig. 444. Stein lamp. Left: Ceramic base with brown and gray grounds; applied handle; multiple shades of painted browns, grays, yellow and white figures of owls; tree branches brown and green; yellow moon on base. Right: Reverse side of milk glass shade and base decorated with a verse from Shakespeare. Base, signed "Handel Ware No. 4029." Drop-in brass font flashed black with copper highlights. Found also without verse and a dark brown ground. Hornet burner; 11" high. *McWright collection. Photo by Frank L. McWright.* $2900

Fig. 445. Stein lamp. Ceramic base; applied handle; milk glass shade and base has a green ground with scenes depicting a rugby match in black; large tasseled pipe on reverse side of base and shade; brass removable oil font. P. & A. Victor burner; 12-3/4" high. *White collection. Photo by Frank L. McWright.* $1225

Fig. 446. Stein lamp. Base has applied handle, with golfing scene in various colors; brass insert removable font. Frosted shade decorated with fleur-de-lis. P. & A. Victor burner; 13-1/4" high. *Rosenberger collection. Photo by David B. Grim.* $420

Fig. 447. Stein lamp. Ceramic base, and milk glass shade in rust, tan and white ground; monk figures in many colors. Tasseled pipe decorations on reverse side of base and shade. Applied handle. Brass removable oil font. Found in other ground colors with different scenes and figures. P. & A. Victor burner; 12-3/4" high. *McWright collection. Photo by Frank L. McWright.* $1200

Fig. 448. Three-tier pedestal lamp pewter woman, balancing embossed elaborately gold font and base. Shade missing. Acorn burner; 8" high. *Solverson collection. Photo by Van Skiver's Studio.* $275

Fig. 449. Square base lamp; enameled flowers and birds in lavender and pink. Shade frosted glass trimmed with delicate flowers in lavender. M.S. with a decoration on wick-raiser. Foreign burner; 11" high. *Caskey collection. Photo by Ramsdell.* $850

Fig. 450. Milk glass; white trimmed in pink and gold with matching colored cupids. Foreign burner; 10-3/4" high. *Schafer collection. Photo by David J. Lans.* $600

Fig. 451. Porcelain lamp; heavily embossed design base with applied handles; multi-colored flowers; matching shade in milk glass. Ca. 1880. See Fig. 615 in book I. P. & A. Victor burner; 9-1/4" high. *Courtesy of Robert W. Skinner Inc.* $580

Fig. 452. White Bristol glass font and shade in a black wrought iron pedestal holder. Foreign burner; 8-1/2" high. *Rosenberger collection. Photo by David B. Grim.* $420

Fig. 453. Pedestal base lamp in pink satin glass; heavily embossed leaf design pattern. A shade has been seen identical in pattern, but slightly smaller in height and width using a nutmeg shade-ring holder, in pink stain, butterscotch satin, blue milk glass, and multi-color painted white milk glass, but not a complete lamp in this size. Hornet burner; 10-1/2" high. *McWright collection. Photo by Frank L. McWright.* $840

Fig. 454. Cased class; chartreuse green; with embossed design. Similar to *Fig.* 569 in book I. Foreign burner: 9" high. *Bailey collection. Photo by Dick Bailey.* $1700

Fig. 455. Satin glass; yellow shading to white; heavily embossed design. (Shade may or may not be original) Brenner burner; 9" high. *Caskey collection. By Ramsdell's Photo.* $465

Fig. 456. Satin glass; pink shading to light; heavily embossed leaf design; embossed ribbing. (Original) Spar Brenner burner; 8-3/4" high. *Carman collection. Logan Photo.* $1650

Fig. 457. Mustard color shading to darker around to top of shade and base; color in shade and base identical and believed to be original. Cased glass with white lining; embossed ribs swirled on base, and vertical on shade. Nutmeg burner; 8-1/4" high. *Author's collection.* $775

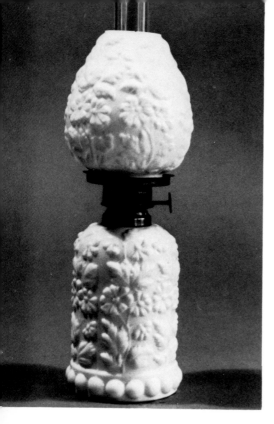

Fig. 458. White milk glass; heavily embossed daisy and leaves design with large dots around bottom. P. & A. Victor burner; 8-1/2" high. *Willis collection. Photo by Cruz Montoya.* $475

Fig. 459. Satin glass lamp; raspberry, embossed pattern. Found in blue shading to light. Foreign burner; 10-1/2" high. *Terrio collection. Photo by Poist's Studio.* $1875

Fig. 460. Bristol white glass; fired on painted flowers and leaves in blue. Foreign burner; 6-3/4" high. *Boles collection.* $370

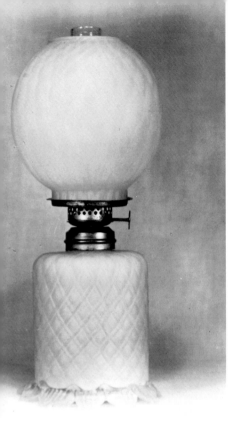

Fig. 461. Yellow satin glass; embossed diamond quilted pattern (cut velvet) applied frosted shell feet. Ca. in the 1920s, or later. Nutmeg burner; 9-1/2" high. Found in blue and orchid. *Clark collection.* $330

Fig. 462. Lavender satin glass; diamond quilted pattern (cut velvet). Frosted edging around top of shade; applied frosted shell petals around bottom of base. Found in yellow and blue. Ca. in the 1920s, or later. Nutmeg burner; 9-1/4" high. *Hulsebus collection. Photo by James Hulsebus.* $330

Fig. 463. Deep green satin glass; embossed diamond quilted pattern (cut velvet). Frosted edging around top of shade; applied frosted shell petals around bottom of base. Found in yellow, blue and orchid. Ca in the 1920s, or later. Nutmeg burner; 9" high. *Cox collection. Photo by Karen & Keith Cox.* $330

Fig. 464. Cased glass; pink shading to lighter pink; embossed design; base like *Fig.* 375 in book I. May or may not be original. Foreign burner; 11-1/2" high. *Oswald collection. Photo by Cliff's Studio.* $300

Fig. 465. Clear glass painted on satin finish decorated to give a semi-frosted look; pink and blue flowers. Foreign burner. 7-7/8" high. *Feltner collection. Photo by David B. Grim.* $500

Fig. 466. Spatter glass in yellow. Nutmeg burner; 8" high. *Willis collection. Photo by Cruz Montoya.* $770

Fig. 467. Pale vaseline glass with white opalescent spots; applied clear glass feet. Large spots are reflections from camera. Nutmeg burner; 7-1/2" high. *Semprini collection. Photo by Frank L. McWright.* $1725

Fig. 468. Spatter glass; soft rose and white; base ribbed swirled. Applied clear glass feet. Shade matching in color may or may not be original. Star Brenner burner; 7" high. *Bartol collection. Photo by Cox Studio.* $550

Fig. 469. Spatter glass; in pink, peach, orange and white with a ribbed swirled pattern. Clear glass applied feet. Foreign burner; 7-1/2" high. *Sandeen collection.* $1300

219

Fig. 470. Green frosted glass lamp; embossed design of flowers. Foreign burner; 6-3/4" high. *Cox collection. Photo by Karen & Keith Cox.* $420

Fig. 471. Log lamp. emerald green glass; base shaped like a tree trunk in textured (rough) embossed glass to simulate tree bark; Matching shade. Foreign burner; 7-1/4" high. *Terrio collection. Photo by Poist's Studio.* $445

Fig. 472. Amber glass with embossed design on pedestal base. Enamel blue and white flowers with green leaves. Hornet burner. 10" high. *Boles collection.* $330

Fig. 473. Pedestal base lamp; cranberry glass, decorated with enameled white flowers. Foreign burner; 6-1/2" high. *Schafer collection. Photo by James Hulsebus.* $525

Fig. 474. Cranberry glass; enameled flowers in pink and blue, green leaves, and white dots. Foreign burner; 9-5/8" high. *McWright collection. Photo by Frank L. McWright.* $625

Fig. 475. Pedestal base; dark aqua (blue) glass; decorated with orange enamel flowers and white leaves. Acorn burner; 8" high. *Cox collection. Photo by Karen & Keith Cox.* $600

Fig. 476. Blue glass decorated with enamel white flowers. Foreign burner; 6-1/2" high. *Boles collection.* $550

Fig. 477. Cranberry glass lamp with enamel yellow decorations; edged with gold. Foreign burner; 6-5/8" high. *McWright collection. Photo by Frank L. McWright.* $650

Fig. 478. Cranberry glass; decorated with opaline flowers and leaves. Foreign burner; 6" high. *Schafer collection. Photo by David J. Lans.* $950

Fig. 479. White overshot; top of shade, font and flowers, clear glass painted lavender to give a transparent look; trimmed in gold. Foreign burner; 7-1/2" high. *Lennox collection. Photo by J.R. Van Schaick.* $750

Fig. 480. Light green iridescent textured glass; painted rose and white flowers; green leaves with gold stems; 6 pointed star on wick-raiser. Foreign burner; 7-1/4" high. *Caskey collection. By Ramsdell's Photo.* $575

Fig. 481. Clear glass flashed with embossed roughness around bottom of base. Background of winter scene in reddish wine. Enameled snow scene in browns, white, and green. Foreign burner; 8-1/2" high. *Boles collection.* $500

Fig. 482. Acid finish glass; embossed floral design brown, green and maroon. Paint not fired on. Matching shade. Foreign burner; 7-1/2" high. *Stewart collection. Photo by Tom Stewart.* $275

Fig. 483. Clear glass lamp, painted light blue to resemble satin. Enameled red tulips, green leaves, and trimmed in gold. Foreign burner; 9" high. *Terrio collection. Photo by Poist's Studio.* $475

Fig. 484. Clear glass with brushed finish, giving a some-what frosted appearance; decorations in gold with tiny red jewels in center of flowers on shade. Base has small turquoise beads at base of central vertical stripes. Applied handle. Design similar to *Fig.* 416 in book I. Foreign burner; 8" high. *Feltner collection. Photo by David B. Grim.* $510

Fig. 485. Amberina glass; inside base, and shade slightly ribbed with a slight swirl. Spots are reflections from camera. Hornet burner; 8" high. *Rodney collection.* $650

Fig. 486. Amber glass lamp. Acorn burner; 6" high. *Plasterer collection. Photo by Poist's Studio.* $375

Fig. 487. Amber glass lamp; blue glass applied handle; enameled orange flowers with blue, green and white leaves. Shade and chimney missing; correct size shade and chimney see *Fig.* 599 in book I. Foreign burner; 3" high. *Plasterer collection. Photo by Poist's Studio.* $185

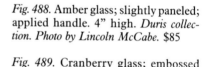

Fig. 488. Amber glass; slightly paneled; applied handle. 4" high. *Duris collection. Photo by Lincoln McCabe.* $85

Fig. 489. Cranberry glass; embossed ribbed and swirled. Hornet burner; 3-1/2" high. *Duris collection. Photo by Lincoln McCabe.* $135

Fig. 490. Cranberry shading to clear glass; embossed shell design with embossed blackberry between; four clear glass shell applied feet. 4-1/2" high. *Duris collection. Photo by Lincoln McCabe.* $150

Fig. 491. Blue glass; harlequin pattern.
3-1/2" high. *Duris collection. Photo by
Lincoln McCabe.* $95

Fig. 492. Amberina glass; quilted pattern; applied clear glass petals around
bottom of base. Found in aqua (blue)
satin glass. Nutmeg burner; 9-1/2"
high. *Cox collection. Photo by Karen &
Keith Cox.* $980

Fig. 493. Amberina glass; faintly paneled; applied crystal petal feet on base.
Nutmeg burner; 8-1/2" high. *Feltner
collection. Photo by David B. Grim.* $1200

Fig. 494. Green glass lamp shading from dark to light green; faintly paneled. Nutmeg burner; 7-1/2" high. *Rosenberger collection. Photo by David B. Grim.* $1050

Fig. 495. Green glass lamp, shading to clear; slightly paneled; embossed shell clear glass applied feet and ornaments on base. Similar to *Fig.* 539 in book I. Found in cranberry glass shading to clear. Nutmeg burner; 7-3/4" high. *Plasterer collection. Photo by Poist's Studio.* $1295

Fig. 496. Cobalt blue glass; enamel decorations in multi-colors; base and shade slightly paneled. Very much like *Fig.* 470 in book I. Nutmeg burner; 7-3/8" high. *Oswald collection. Photo by Cliff's Studio.* $500

Fig. 497. Amber glass; similar in size and shape as "Nellie Bly" in Fig. 219 in book I. Hornet burner; 9" high. *Stewart collection. Photo by Tom Stewart.* $315

Fig. 498. Crystal stem pedestal base lamp with teal blue font and matching bulbous chimney. Foreign burner; 11-1/4" high. *Feltner collection. Photo by David B. Grim.* $370

Fig. 499. Cranberry glass; diamond quilted pattern. "French". Foreign burner; 6-3/4" high. *Schafer collection. Photo by David J. Lans.* $800

Fig. 500. Cranberry glass; diamond and tear-drop pattern. Foreign burner; 6-3/4" high. *Cox collection. Photo by Karen & Keith Cox.* $900

Fig. 501. Opalescent vaseline lamp with gold decorations largely worn off. Acorn burner; 6-1/4" high. *Author's collection.* $425

Fig. 502. White opalescent bristol glass; blue glass applied decoration on sides; blue glass band around top of chimney-shade. In Burley and Tyrrell Co., Chicago 1907 catalog shown with identical burners on "Japanese Decorated" lamps. Made in Japan. Olmsted type burner; 5-3/4" high. *Author's collection. Photo by Poist's Studio.* $510

Fig. 503. Cranberry glass; white opalescent swirls. (Believed to be old) Nutmeg burner: 7-3/4" high. *Bailey collection. Photo by Dick Bailey.* $425

Fig. 504. Hand lamp; clear opalescent glass with inverted swirl stripes, matching shade; clear glass applied handle. Hornet burner; 6-3/4" high. *Semprini collection. Photo by Frank L. McWright.* $735

Fig. 505. Cranberry glass with opalescent swirls; spots are reflections from camera. Nutmeg burner; 7" high. *Stewart collection. Photo by Tom Stewart.* $1600

Fig. 506. Cranberry glass; pink opalescent stripes. Star on wick-raiser. Foreign burner; 8-3/4" high. *Bartol collection. Photo by Cox Studio.* $1200

Fig. 507. Amber glass with honey swirl striped pattern; applied glass peach color feet. Similar to *Fig.* 543 in book I. *Caskey collection. By Ramsdell's Photo.* $500

Fig. 508. White opalescent glass lamp with clear eyes. (Sometimes called "Thousand eyes or Honeycomb".) Nutmeg burner; 7-1/2" high. *Author's collection.* $1100

Fig. 509. Iridescent glass; dark pink fading to white. Foreign burner: 9-1/2" high. *Cox collection. Photo by Karen & Keith Cox.* $1400

Fig. 510. Opalescent vaseline glass; satin finish; swirl pattern. Foreign burner; 9-5/16" high. *Feltner collection. Photo by David B. Grim.* $1050

Fig. 511. Opalescent glass; blue-white faintly paneled with applied heavy roll around top of font. Foreign burner; 7-1/2" high. *McWright collection. Photo by Frank L. McWright.* $770

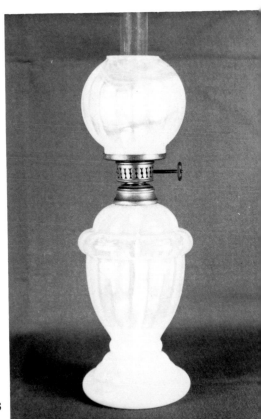

Fig. 512. Vasa Marrhina glass. Clear with blue, pink, green, and silver spatters. Spar Brenner burner; 8-1/2" high. *Boles collection.* $790

Fig. 513. Clear glass; blue shading to light; slightly embossed swirl; applied clear glass shell petals around base. Foreign burner; 9-3/4" high. *Boles collection.* $900

Fig. 514. Cranberry glass, shading to clear in an embossed ribbed swirl pattern. White enameled flowers and gold vines. Foreign burner; 10" high. *Boles collection.* $1100

Fig. 515. Vasa Marrhina base mottled in rust, white and silver; embossed amber swirl shade; marked M.S. with decoration wick-raiser. (Shade may or may not be original.) Foreign burner; 10-1/2" high. *Caskey collection. By Ramsdell's Photo.* $345

Fig. 516. Bright orange cased glass lamp; ornamented with dark orange and white "Frosting" decorating the base and shade. Similar to color plate XLIV, but "Frosting" different. Foreign burner; 9-1/4" high. *Cox collection. Photo by Karen & Keith Cox.* $825

Fig. 517. Satin glass; dark chartreuse (green) shading to light. Melon ribbed swirled with embossed leaf design. Foreign burner; 9" high. *Cox collection. Photo by Karen & Keith Cox.* $1600

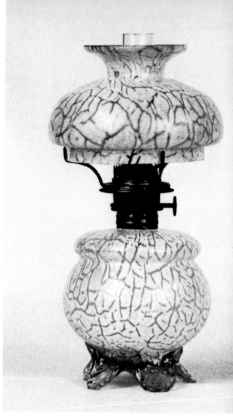

Fig. 518. Parian, white glass with embossed design trimmed in gold; gold partly worn off. Nutmeg burner; 7-1/2" high. *Schafer collection. Photo by David J. Lans.* $1125

Fig. 519. Amber glass with white crackle overlay. Applied amber shell feet. Probably wrong shade holder. Nutmeg burner; 8-1/4" high. *Schafer collection. Photo by David J. Lans.* $2225

Fig. 520. Cranberry glass; embossed diamond pattern; applied clear glass feet. Nutmeg burner; 8-1/2" high. *Semprini collection. Photo by Frank L. McWright.* $1525

Fig. 521. Amber glass; honeycomb pattern. Applied feet. Nutmeg burner; 6" high. *Schafer collection. Photo by David J. Lans.* $840

Fig. 522 Basket-weave base with applied handle in bisque; embossed fired-on painted colorful decorations around top and on handle. Blue satin glass; diamond-of-pearl pattern shade. Shade like *Fig.* 599 in book I. Supposed to be original. Foreign burner; 5-1/2" high. *Schafer collection. Photo by David J. Lans.* $575

Fig. 523. Pink glass lamp, in cased in silver filigree medallion design pattern. Nutmeg burner; 7-1/4" high. *Sandeen collection.* $2500

Fig. 524. Satin glass mother-of-pearl; light blue, raindrop pattern. Frosted, applied shell feet. Wrong shade holder. Nutmeg burner; 8-1/2" high. *Boles collection.* $2440

Fig. 525. Blue satin glass lamp; enameled decorations in blue, gold, and pink. Nutmeg burner; 8-1/2" high. *Author's collection.* $2500

Fig. 526. Burmese color satin glass with enamel decorations. Similar to *Fig.* 575 in book I. Foreign burner; 8-1/2" high. *Schafer collection. Photo by David J. Lans.* $1800

Fig. 527. Satin Fireglow glass lamp. The glass is described as brownish-pink, although there are some variations of brown and white. Many claim Sandwich made the glass, others credit it to some European manufacturer. There is no assurance where it was made. It seems to be related to Burmese decorations similar to Fig. 574 in book I. "Korner & Co., Berlin" marked burner; 7-1/4" high. *Author's collection.* $2625

Fig. 528. Fireglow satin glass. Fired on paint decorations in brown. Marked "Korner & Co., Berlin" burner; 7-1/2" high. *Terrio collection.* $2625

Fig. 529. Blue satin glass with colorful birds, leaves, flowers and berries. Possibly Web. English burner: 6-1/2" high. *Schafer collection. Photo by David J. Lans.* $1575

Fig. 530. Cream ground; satin glass with rust leaves and branches. Possibly Webb. English burner; 7-3/4" high. *Schafer collection. Photo by David J. Lans.* $1575

Fig. 531. Burmese glass; decorated in brown, green, red, and pale blue. Signed on bottom, Thomas Webb (Wrong shade holder.) Foreign burner: 11-1/4" high. *Rodney collection.* $3450

Fig. 532. Mother-of-pearl satin glass; pink shading to lighter; diamond quilted pattern; decorated with coralene on base and shade; applied frosted feet; ornamental decoration on wick-raiser. Foreign burner; 10" high. *Caskey collection. By Ramsdell's Photo.* $5580

Fig. 533. Mother-of-pearl satin glass; diamond quilted pattern; rose color with frosted applied feet. Kosmos Brenner burner; 8-3/4" high. *Caskey collection. By Ramsdell's Photo.* $3000

Fig. 534. Satin glass; mother-of-pearl; diamond pattern in yellow. Frosted applied feet. Nutmeg burner; 9-1/2" high. *Bailey collection. Photo by Dick Bailey.* $3300

Fig. 535. Blue frosted overshot glass; six applied clear glass petal feet. Foreign burner; 6" high. *Cox collection. Photo by Karen & Keith Cox.* $1350

Fig. 536. Satin glass; mother-of-pearl diamond pattern; melon ribbed; frosted glass shell applied feet; pink shading to light. Spar Brenner burner; 9-1/2" high. *Carman collection. Logan Photo.* $3000

Fig. 537. Overshot glass; vaseline with ruffled shade. Applied glass shell feet. Foreign burner; 8-1/2" high. *Reith collection. Photo by Michael Clifton.* $1725

Fig. 538. Pink opalescent threaded glass; heavily ribbed, with clear glass applied loop handles; applied clear glass petal or "shell" feet. Top of shade and loop handles unlike *Fig. 539.* Foreign burner; 11-1/2" high. *Terrio collection.* $2075

Fig. 539. Threaded glass; pink opalescent; heavily ribbed; applied crystal loop handles; applied crystal petal feet. Top of shade and loop handles unlike Fig. 538. Foreign burner; 11-1/4" high. *McWright collection. Photo by Frank L. McWright.* $2075

Fig. 540. Opalescent glass; ribbed swirled design; pink shading to light; applied clear glass handles; applied pink flower with applied green leaves. Foreign burner; 8-3/4" high. *Cox collection. Photo by Karen & Keith Cox.* $2650

Fig. 541. Cameo lamp; satin glass raspberry color with applied white floral decorations. Flowers on base and shade do not match, but color is identical. Ring for holding shade on burner is missing. P. & A. Victor burner; 8-1/4" high. *Author's collection.* $10,500

Fig. 542. Verre Moire (Nailsea) in pink and white with frosted applied flowers, stems, and feet. Foreign burner; 11" high. *Boles collection.* $5000

Fig. 543. 3-tier lamp on iron base painted black; pink cased fonts with frosted petal shades. On wick-turner "The P & A Mfg Co," which also made the Acorn, Nutmeg, and Hornet. Saw another lamp identical with same shades except it had blue fonts, so the lamp must be original. P & A burners; 12-1/2" high. *Author's collection.* $1350

Fig. 544. Cranberry glass; enameled decorations in gold, green and white. Burner same size as *Fig.* 599 in book I. Foreign burner: 5-3/4" high. *Author's collection.* $1000

Fig. 545. Clear glass with pressed rose design painted in rose and gold. This glass is usually called "Goofus". Paint not fired on, often partly or entirely missing. Hornet burner; 12-1/4" high. *Author's collection.* $175

Fig. 546. Cranberry glass; enameled decorations in gold, blue and white. Nutmeg burner: 5-3/4" high. *Author's collection.* $675

Fig. 547. Cut glass; strawberry pattern; rainbow coloring. Applied silver band, and ball feet around bottom of base. Foreign burner; 8-1/2" high. *Author's collection.* $10,000

Fig. 548. Spatter glass; white ground with shades of reddish browns. Clear glass applied feet. Acorn burner; 7-1/2" high. *Author's collection.* $1800

Fig. 549. Mother-of-pearl satin glass in diamond pattern; dark pink shading to light. applied frosted satin ribbed handle. Foreign burner; 8-1/2" high. *Author's collection.* $5250

Fig. 550. Cased glass; end-of-day predominately orange, pink, and white. Embossed Acanthus pattern with a swirl. Nutmeg burner; 8" high. *Author's collection.* $1700

Fig. 551. Porcelain base with applied Colonial man and woman at sides holding a garland of flowers between them, pink wash, touches of gold; milk glass shade with over-painted sprays of flowers. Foreign burner. 11-3/4" to top of shade. *Feltner collection.* $500

Fig. 552. Bisque girl and cart with pink and blue accents, pink bisque shade with three applied cherubs. Base like Fig. 342 in book II. Sparr Brenner burner. 9-1/2" to top of shade. Shade very rare. *Feltner collection.* $200

Fig. 553. Bisque cherub supporting a beribboned and netted sheaf. Usual bristol shade used for many figurals. Kosmos-Brenner burner. 5" to top of collar. *Feltner collection.* $600

Fig. 554. Delft porcelain, fired on painted boat scenes in blue, darker blue decorations. On bottom of base 3. Sparr Brenner burner. 8-1/4" high. *Nesses collection.* $400

Fig. 555. Tan and dark brown begging Pug dog. Green ball shade not original. Foreign burner. 6-1/4" to top of collar. *Feltner collection.* $1000

Fig. 556. White poodle sitting on pink base, blue collar, excellent detail from teeth right on down to toenails, rampant gold lion on clambroth shade. Wick turner marked "Prince & Symons, Lion Lamp Works, London, Manufactured in Germany." 9" to top of collar. *Feltner collection.* $1225

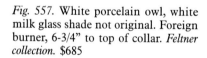

Fig. 557. White porcelain owl, white milk glass shade not original. Foreign burner, 6-3/4" to top of collar. *Feltner collection.* $685

Fig. 558. Owl lamp in sapphire blue shading to clear at bottom. Shade and base original. Also base made in rainbow cased glass. Sparr Brenner burner. 5-1/4" to top of collar. *Feltner collection.* $1300

Fig. 559. Green porcelain owl, white milk glass shade. French, foreign burner. 6-1/4" to top of collar. *Feltner collection.* $700

Fig. 560. White bristol-type glass lamp, old fashion Gibson girl dressed in bloomers and hat standing along side of bicycle. Fired on paint in blue. Acorn burner. 9" high. *Smith collection.* $1100

Fig. 561. White bristol-type glass lamp, fired on painted faintly blue around top and bottom of base. Windmill scene in darker blue. Prima-Rund Brenner burner. 10" high. *Smith collection.* $1300

Fig. 562. White mother-of-pearl glass lamp with applied frosted feet. Note: The shade on this lamp is questionable. Several have examined the shade with a magnifying glass, the edges of the openings are rolled out as if they overlapped the mole. If the openings were broken and filed, the openings would be smooth and not overlapped. A dealer saw a lamp identical to this one in blue. The lamp is old; it would be interesting to know if someone else ever saw a shade with openings like in this one, similar to Fig. 602 in book I. Nutmeg burner. 8-3/4" high. *Nesses collection.* $1525 if original.

Fig. 563. Heavy clear glass base with ball shade; remnants of unfired painted flowers; reverse embossed design in foot. 7-1/8" to top of shade. *Feltner collection.* $100

Fig. 565. Pewter pedestal lamp with original shade. French marked "Lampe Titus." Foreign burner. 5-1/2" to top of shade. *Feltner collection.* $130

Fig. 564. Cranberry glass, faintly swirl-ribbed in base and shade. Not very old, becoming very collectible. Similar to Fig. 503 in book II. Nutmeg burner. 8-3/4" high. *Nesses collection.* $300

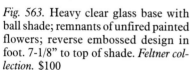

Fig. 566. Brass pedestal lamp with heavily embossed font, green milk glass shade like Fig. 101 in book I. Nutmeg burner. 7-3/4" to top of shade. *Feltner collection.* $160

Bibliography

Anonymous, "Miniature Lamps." *Spinning Wheel*, December 1958.

____, Novelties in Night Lamps." *Spinning Wheel*," October 1962.

____, "Miniature Lamps, a Pictorial Study." *Spinning Wheels*, December 1966.

____, Notices of Judgement 1930-1931 (Food and Drug Cases). Washington.

____, Patent Records. U.S. Patent Office. Washington.

Barbour, Harriot Buxton, *Sandwich the Town that Glass Built. Boston*

Barbour, Harriot Buxton, *Sandwich the Town that Glass Built.* Boston 1948.

Cole, Ann Kilborn. "Lamps in Miniature." *Philadelphia Inquirer Magazine*, January 24, 1960.

Dozois, Dorothea Ann. "New Interest in Old Lamps." *Hobbies*, November 1947.

Freeman, Larry. *Light on Old Lamps*. Watkins Glen, N.Y. 1946.

Giddens, Paul H. *Early Days of Oil*. Princeton, N.J. 1946.

Hayward, Arthur H. *Colonial Lighting*. Boston 1923.

Kamm, Minnie Watson. Pitcher Books (Nos. 1-8). Detroit 1939-1954.

Lee, Ruth Webb. *Sandwich Glass* 8th ed. Northborough, Mass. 1947.

Peterson, Arthur G. *Salt and Salt Shakers*. Washington 1960.

Revi, Albert Christian. *Nineteenth Century Glass*. New York 1959.

Smith, Frank. R. & Ruth E. *Miniature Lamps*. Thomas Nelson & Sons, New York 1968.

Thwing, Leroy, Flickering Flames. *A History of Domestic Lighting Through the Ages*. Rutland, Vt. 1958.

Watkins, C. Malcolm. *Artificial Lighting in America* 1830-1860 Washington 1951.

Other Schiffer Titles

Miniature Victorian Lamps Marjorie Hulsebus. Miniature oil lamps are beautiful reminders of Victorian days, in glass, china, porcelain, brass, and silver. Styles range from the delicacy of the Victorian parlor through Art Nouveau elegance. This reference features almost 450 lamps never before seen in any book, with color photos and detailed information including a useful Price Guide.
Size: 6" x 9"   450 lamps   192 pp.
Price Guide/Index
ISBN: 0-88740-931-8   hard cover $39.95

Lamps of the '50s & '60s Jan Lindenberger. New lamp styles represent one of the offbeat fruits of the distinct American postwar culture. Revisit the lamps we loved to hate, like amoeba, starburst, atomic, the indomitable lava lamps, figural TV lamps and a generous sampling of floor and table designs. Each lamp is illustrated in color with a current market value to aid collectors.
Size: 6" x 9"   251 color photos   144 pp.
Price Guide
ISBN: 0-7643-0355-4   soft cover $16.95

50s TV Lamps Calvin Shepherd. Nearly 400 color photos explore the many forms of TV lamps. In the early days of television, people attempted to protect themselves from the new machines with creative lamps that provided back light that was believed to protect the eyes. These lamps took on fantastic forms and sometimes doubled as vases or planters.
Size: 8.5" x 11"   395 color photos   128 pp.
Price Guide
ISBN: 0-7643-0601-4   soft cover $24.95

The Glass Industry in Sandwich, Lighting Devices Volume 2 Raymond E. Barlow & Joan E. Kaiser. Sandwich glass lighting devices and accessories in great detail.
Size: 9" x 12"   476 color photos   300 pp.
Glossary, Index
ISBN: 0-88740-170-8   hard cover $95.00

Antique Lamp Buyer's Guide, Identifyin **Late 19th and Early 20th Century America** **Lighting** *Revised & Expanded 2nd Edition* Nadj Maril. Many basic questions confronting an tique lamp buyers, from "Where do I look for manufacturer's signature?" to "How do I dis tinguish reproductions from originals?" ar answered here. Using color photographs an catalogue illustrations, a wealth of informatio is presented including buying or selling ol lighting, restoration issues like rewiring, prac tical uses for fixtures originally made for gas o oil, and restoring and protecting metal finishes
Size: 8 1/2" x 11"   200 illus.   144 pp
Revised Price Guide/Index
ISBN: 0-7643-0854-8   soft cover $29.9.

Popular '50s and '60s Glass, Color Along th **River** Leslie Piña. Commerical glass productio along the Ohio River Valley in the 1950s an 1960s by companies such as Blenko, Pilgrim Rainbow, Viking, Kanawaha, Bischiff Morgantown and others that made free- an mold-blown production glass in modern, some times bizarre, shapes and wildly vibrant colors The book has over 400 color photos of the beau tiful glass, its labels, catalog pages, and com pany histories.
Size: 8 1/2" x 11"   409 color photos   176 pp
Price Guide
ISBN: 0-88740-829-X   hard cover $29.9

Tiffin Glass, 1914–1940 Leslie Piña & Jerry Gallagher. Tiffin was one of the giants of Ameri can glassmaking. This is the first book to present all color photos of hundreds of Tiffin' products. Vases, bowls, and candlesticks in wide variety of colors and styles, from commor to rare, are all in this book, with large section devoted to Tiffin's pressed satin glass, lamps and baskets.
Size: 8 1/2" x 11"   527 color photos   160 pp
Price Guide/Index
ISBN: 0-7643-0102-0   hard cover $29.95